Welcome to...

HOME-BASED
BUSINESS
COMPUTING

Welcome to...

HOME-BASED
BUSINESS
COMPUTING

L.R. Shannon
& Janet Shannon

MIS:
PRESS

A Subsidiary of
Henry Holt and Co., Inc.

First Edition—1995

```
Shannon, L.R.
    Welcome to- home-based business computing / L.R. Shannon  &
  Janet Shannon.
       p.   cm.
    Includes index.
    ISBN 1-55828-403-6
    1. Telecommuting.   2. Home-based businesses.
    3. Microcomputers-Purchasing.  I. Shannon, Janet.  II. Title.
  HD2333.S53  1995
  658'.041--dc20                                     94-46464
                                                       CIP
```

Printed in the United States of America.

10 9 8 7 6 5 4 3 2 1

MIS:Press books are available at special discounts for bulk purchases for sales promotions, premiums, fund-raising, or educational use. Special editions or book excerpts can also be created to specification.

Trademarks

Throughout this book, trademarked names are used. Rather than put a trademark symbol after every occurrence of a trademarked name, we used the names in an editorial fashion only, and to the benefit of the trademark owner, with no intention of infringement of the trademark. Where such designations appear in this book, they have been printed with initial caps.

Editor-in-Chief: Paul Farrell
Managing Editor: Cary Sullivan
Development Editor: Judy Brief
Production Editor: Joe McPartland
Copy Editor: Gwynne Jackson

DEDICATION

For Careen and Patrick

CONTENTS

CHAPTER 2: THE SOFT PART............ 31

CHAPTER 3: GETTING ORGANIZED 53

CHAPTER 4: THE HARD PART AGAIN 83

CHAPTER 5: THE SOFT PART AGAIN 97

CHAPTER 6: BUYING SMART 115

CHAPTER 7: STAYING SMART 135

CHAPTER 8: THE REST OF YOUR LIFE 157

APPENDIX A: KEYBOARD SHORTCUTS 173

APPENDIX B: RECOMMENDED HARDWARE 177

APPENDIX C: RECOMMENDED SOFTWARE 181

APPENDIX D: RECOMMENDED BOOKS AND MAGAZINES 187

APPENDIX E: HISTORY 189

GLOSSARY 195
INDEX 211

ACKNOWLEDGMENTS

Thanks to Judy Brief, Joe McPartland, Fauzia Burke, and the rest of the staff at MIS:Press for help in developing, designing and marketing the book.

Thanks also to Steve Luciani and Bob Harris of *The New York Times* for their help and technical support.

INTRODUCTION

WHY AM I READING THIS?

You are a middle-class American as the 1990s lurch incredibly into the 2000s, and you are not going to let the bastards wear you down.

The home office is a '90s dream. You make your living without catering to an inept boss. You are the boss, and you are definitely ept. You don't have to commute. You walk upstairs or downstairs, or to the next room, and you are on the job. You set your own hours. If a great idea strikes at 3 in the morning, you deal with it. If that idea doesn't look nearly so great at 2 the next afternoon, you change or abandon it. You care for the kids, do an errand in the middle of the day, invite a neighbor in for coffee, dash out a memo on the beach or by the pool. You are featured in the better class of supermarket magazines. It's a lovely dream.

Sure.

On the other hand, maybe your company has been "downsized"—made more efficient by firing everybody who isn't related to the CEO or knows where he keeps the real set of books—and you can't find another regular job. You care for the kids because you can't afford to pay anyone else to do it for you. You don't know of anybody desperately poor enough or unfortunate enough to run other people's errands, the neighbors are at work in conventional offices, with generous salaries and long paid vacations and sick days for the sniffles, and if there were a beach nearby the sand and salt water and sun would lead to sunburn, which leads to cancer, which leads to death, which otherwise you would escape.

Sure.

TOWARD A HOME OFFICE

Maybe the home office isn't a full-time workplace yet. You are an accountant in a downtown high-rise, and you do tax returns at home for friends or friends of friends and concoct the books for three neighborhood shops. Maybe you are a part-time travel agent in a mall storefront, with half a dozen private outside clients. Or you teach English as a second language by day; by night, you write articles for the local newspaper and the state's magazine. Whatever, you do it many weekday hours. Whatever else, you do it evenings and hours off. The extra money is nice, almost necessary, the business would grow if you could handle it, and the sense of security and independence is beyond measure.

You are a person with skills and energy trying to live a decent life in a decade that doesn't make it easy. You are not much interested in computers for themselves, only as a way to get the job done. Probably you already use a computer, at home or on the main job, or know that you should, just as you have a machine that answers the household phone when you are in the office or out shopping and another that reheats the pizza that was delivered too late. But there must be a better way, both for now and as a path into the future.

Here are some ideas. Don't take them all too seriously, and certainly not all at once, but do read on. You might learn something; we did.

The home office is a space at home (you figured that out) where you do a substantial amount of paid work, ranging from a corner of the bedroom or dining area to a dedicated room. This book concentrates on mechanical ways to increase "productivity," a tiring word that just means getting more work done in the same amount of time, or the same amount of work done in less time. Bosses love that word. Well, when you are your own boss, you love it too. A home office built around the wrong computer and accessories can complicate your life enormously. Believe us, we know. The right ones can pay you back time and time again. Getting paid back is what it's all about.

COMPUTERIZING YOUR HOME OFFICE

This book is written under the assumption that you are using, or will buy, a computer running Microsoft Windows 3.1 or later or a Macintosh running System 7.1 or later. This is not necessarily a safe assumption—there are many other computers, both old and new, running many other systems, both old and new, and the book can be helpful to people who own them. But the line had to be drawn somewhere.

WHAT IT ALL MEANS

PC, short for personal computer, stands for the personal computers made by IBM and the hundreds of other personal computers compatible with the IBMs but made by Compaq, Packard Bell, Zenith, NEC, AST, Canon, Dell, Gateway, Zeos, two kids named Steve in the garage next door, and uncountable other companies.

Although Macintoshes, made by the Apple Corporation, are also personal computers, they will not be called PCs here, but Macintoshes or Macs. At this writing, Macintoshes are made only by Apple. But, like everything else in this unmatched industry, that is subject to rapid change.

Scattered here and there are boxes that define technical terms we didn't want to explain in the main text, or that you can ignore although you shouldn't, as well as strategies, examples, several odds, and a few ends. The glossary repeats those definitions in case you have to look them up later, as well as terms that were defined in the main text because they couldn't be avoided and a few that don't appear there at all. There are appendixes that list the products mentioned in the text and standard keyboard shortcuts for Windows and the Macintosh. There are also lots of digressions.

Nowhere is there advice on how you should run your business. You know how to do that and we don't.

HOW THIS BOOK IS ORGANIZED

CHAPTER 1—THE HARD PART

The basic parts of a home-office computer, desktop or portable. Monitor and main box, disk drives and keyboard, mouse and modem, and printer. A second computer. Tying them together.

CHAPTER 2—THE SOFT PART

Essential software to get the job done. The system: a PC running Windows or a Macintosh running System 7. Integrated software that can do several jobs. Word processors. Spreadsheets. Database managers. Graphics programs. Communications programs. Printer programs.

CHAPTER 3—GETTING ORGANIZED

Arranging a computer-centered home office. Both the physical office, the stuff on the floor and against the walls, and the mental office, the stuff in the computer and in your head. Designing the space and spending the money right. Comfort, efficiency, health, and safety.

CHAPTER 4—THE HARD PART AGAIN

Equipment you didn't know you needed, but might. Specialized stuff like sound cards, speakers, scanners, extra hard drives, and tape backups.

CHAPTER 5—THE SOFT PART AGAIN

Software you didn't know you needed, but might. Specialized stuff like business letters on disk, publicity guides, foreign-language aids, and makeup for your interface.

CHAPTER 6—BUYING SMART

How to read a computer ad. Buying what you need at a price you can afford. Mail order or superstores? Stealing software. Technical support.

CHAPTER 7—STAYING SMART

Keeping up without making a career out of it. Reading, both on paper and on-line.

CHAPTER 8—THE REST OF YOUR LIFE

Having fun with the computer.

APPENDIX A

Keyboard shortcuts.

APPENDIX B

Recommended hardware for PCs and Macs.

APPENDIX C

Recommended software for PCs and Macs.

APPENDIX D

Books and magazines.

APPENDIX E

History.

GLOSSARY

INDEX

THE HARD PART

TO DO LIST

✓ Monitors
✓ Computer systems, both desktop and portable
✓ Keyboards
✓ Printers
✓ Mice
✓ Modems

It's a damned shame, but you have to learn a little about hardware to operate a computer effectively. Sorry, but a bit of bother now saves a lot of bother later.

Learning the right names of things is a big part, perhaps the biggest part, of becoming a human being, so much so that we often don't think about it. You would think about it, though, if you had to tell the garage mechanic that "the doohickey I step on to stop the car is broken" or to tell your spouse that "that bunch of red things in your hand sure smells sweet" or to ask the bartender for a shot of "the clear stuff in the green bottle." If you already know a little bit about hardware, turn to the Buying Guide at the end of the chapter and see if you understand it. Or just skip the whole chapter and, if you get stuck later, come back here or consult the glossary in the back of the book, which reproduces the definitions scattered on the pages where they are needed, plus the ones in the main text.

What is *hardware*, anyway? It is the computer equivalent of the stuff you buy in a regular hardware store—screwdrivers, saws, lawn mowers, and plungers. The computer sitting, or soon to be sitting, on your desk is hardware. You can scratch it, lift it, pet it. You may often want to kick it, but don't, at least not when it is on.

From the top down, most computers consist of a monitor; the main box, which is the computer itself; a keyboard, and, off to the side, a mouse or trackball. Other pieces of hardware may also be attached, and we'll get to them sooner or later, and some of the separate units already mentioned may be combined. All of these things together, built in or separate, comprise a *personal computer system*.

Personal computer systems, which have existed for fewer than 20 years, are the most empowering, versatile, useful, complex, intelligent, enhancing, and maddening inventions ever seen. If you are old enough to remember the first digital computers, behemoths that lumbered into our lives toward the end of World War II, you may recall the term "electronic brain" and, a little later, cards with holes in them that were not to be folded, spindled, or mutilated. Well, if you have an ordinary calculator on your desk or in your pocket, treat it with more respect. It is far brainier than Univac or Eniac ever dreamed of being. The computer that guided the lunar module to the first landing on the moon wasn't as smart as the Compaq or Macintosh on which you prepare invoices.

Let's start with the basic hardware, from the top, one piece at a time.

MONITOR

This is the television set on which you view not reruns of *I Love Lucy* or movies that would have been shown in seedy downtown theaters a few years ago, but the words you type, the mailing lists and budgets you work with, all the information that makes up your business. The monitor is also called the screen, or display, or sometimes the CRT, for cathode-ray tube, or VDT, for video display terminal, by people who want to sound important and knowing, or who really are important and knowing. Learn half a dozen terms like those and you, too, can bore people at cocktail parties or church potlucks.

Monitors come in two styles you already know about and two you may not know about. The two you know about are black and white and color, although that looks like three. The other two are VGA and SVGA.

WHAT IT ALL MEANS

VGA

Video Graphics Array, a standard in PC monitors and their associated internal computer circuitry, that offers a resolution of 640 by 480 pixels. The term is not ordinarily applied to Macintosh monitors, most of which do offer at least the same resolution standard.

continued...

SVGA

Super You Know What, which offers a resolution of 800 by 600 pixels, or 1024 by 768, or even more. It is crisper than regular VGA, but also slower, unless you have more powerful gear than you need for VGA.

PIXEL

A *picture element*, one of the dots that the letters, numbers, squares, and circles on the screen are made of.

DOT PITCH

The spacing of the dots.

INTERLACED, NONINTERLACED

An interlaced monitor paints only half the screen at a time—every other line—and then it goes back and does the other half. It may flicker, either visibly or subliminally, and the flickering can tire your eyes even if they can't see it. A noninterlaced monitor doesn't paint only half the screen at a time, and consequently doesn't flicker or streak.

BLACK AND WHITE

Also called *monochrome*, black and white sounds simple, but nothing about computers is that simple or you wouldn't be reading a book about them. For one thing, the screen may show more or less black letters and numbers on a more or less white screen, or more or less white letters and numbers on a more or less black screen, not to mention that the "black" may be green or amber. A monochrome monitor can go either way, white on black or black on white, depending on the software (Chapter 2) the computer is taking its orders from. For another thing, the black-and-white monitor may really be a *gray-scale* monitor. That is a monitor that translates colors into shades of gray, from as few as 4 shades to as many as 256. Truly black-and-white displays are rare these days and were always unattractive. Gray-scale displays are pretty nice, although color is better.

COLOR

Color is not as simple as it sounds either. Everything said about black and white applies to color. There can be from 4 to 256 colors, just like shades of gray, and indeed there can be zillions if you have an irresistible yen for them and your credit card is platinum. There are VGA color monitors, and SVGA color monitors; SVGA is better than VGA, but VGA is okay. Buy VGA if you must, SVGA if you can. Don't settle for anything less than VGA.

Get color if you possibly can, even if you think you don't need it. You can run a color monitor as a black-and-white or gray-scale monitor, and you might want to sometimes because everything happens faster in black and white, but you can't run a black-and-white or gray-scale monitor as a color monitor no matter how much you yearn to see the losses for the last quarter in truly red ink.

Besides, games look much better in color. Don't try to kid us, or yourself; you *will* play games on your computer (see Figure 1.1). In fact, you *should* play games, for reasons we may remember to get around to later.

SCREEN SIZE

Monitors, like television sets, come with screens of different sizes, and like television sets, bigger screens cost more than smaller ones. Any size monitor also costs more than the same size television set, because monitors have to be sharper, and manufacturers don't sell nearly as many of them as they do television sets.

The standard size screen on a computer monitor is 14 inches from one corner to the diagonally opposite corner, although the manufacturers cheat in this as they do in many other things by measuring the tube before it is put in the case, which cuts off a little of the area. A 15-inch screen is noticeably bigger for mathematical reasons that we won't trouble you with, even if we could, and a 13-inch screen is noticeably smaller. Then there are 17-inch and 21-inch screens, which are wonderfully bigger if you need them and can afford to spend the money and give up the space.

- A rich guy with poor eyesight might want a 21-inch monitor
- Or someone who does a lot of graphics work and has to see the details
- Or someone who needs or likes to keep three or four different programs running and easily available
- Or someone who shows his work to clients on the screen rather than as a printed copy.

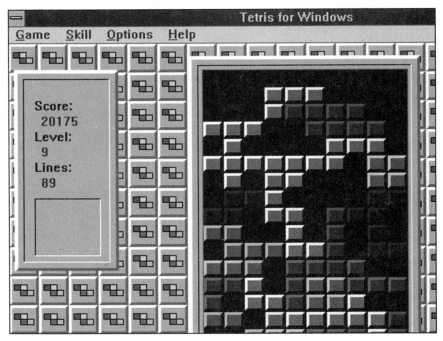

Figure 1.1 Tetris is one of the addicting computer games that can keep you away from your work.

For most of us, though, a 13-inch or 14-inch or 15-inch screen will do just fine, and since we won't be sitting much farther away from a 21-inch screen than from a 14-inch one the big picture can be overwhelming.

RESOLUTION AND DOT PITCH

There are two other technicalities we might as well get out of the way here. At a minimum, the resolution of a 13-, 14-, or 15-inch monitor, in combination with the circuit card in the computer, should be 640 by 480 pixels (larger numbers are better, especially in big monitors), which is what VGA is anyway, and the dot pitch should be 0.28 millimeter (larger numbers are worse in regular-sized monitors). The display should not be interlaced; it should be noninterlaced.

MAIN BOX

More often called the computer or system box (or wrongly, the CPU), this is the heart of the system. It is a container usually placed horizontally on the desk with the monitor on top of it, although it may be a vertical unit next to the monitor on the desk or on the floor where the cat can get at it and ruin it with hairballs. Everything—monitor, keyboard, cat, mouse, printer—is attached to it. On the outside are openings into which floppy disks or CD-ROMs are inserted. On the inside are the hard disk, the chips that run the computer and remember what's going on, and a load of other electrical equipment. Now to deal with the mess inside the box one step at a time.

FLOPPY DISK DRIVES

Floppy disks are round pieces of material, much like recording tape, that are thin enough to be floppy if you take them out of their cases, which you should never do. The disks that are 3.5 inches in diameter, the most common kind, are enclosed in a rectangular plastic case, so they are neither floppy nor disklike on the outside, but they are on the inside, as you can see if you take a look, which you should also never do.

The other kind are 5.25 inches in diameter, and neither floppy nor disk-shaped if you take them out of their outer thin-paper envelopes, which you have to do, and both floppy and disk-shaped if you take them out of their inner stiff-paper envelopes, which you should, again, never do.

The 3.5-inch disks fit into 3.5-inch drives through an opening just big enough to hold them on the outside front (always on the outside, usually on the front) of the computer, and the 5.25-inch disks fit into their spot on the always outside usually front face of the computer (see Figure 1.2 for a sample of both disk types).

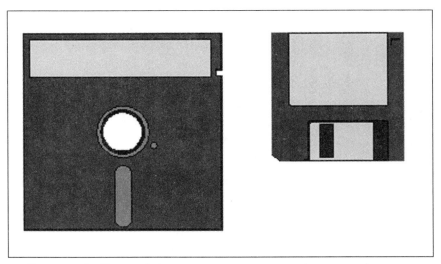

Figure 1.2 Floppy disks come in two sizes and pretty colors, too.

When you ask for a piece of information that is stored on a floppy disk, it spins until a tiny head beneath it finds what you are looking for. When you tell the computer to store information on a floppy disk, it spins until the tiny head finds a place or places to put it. (The head is part of the drive, the mechanical device in the main box, not the floppy disk itself.) Not all PCs take both sizes of floppy disks, and Macs take only 3.5-inch disks. If your PC can take only one size, it should be the 3.5-inch one, which stores more information than the 5.25-inch size and is handier besides.

In the real world, a quart bottle holds more milk than a pint bottle, but in the computer world it is the other way around. Both sizes (disks, not bottles) store about a million characters, called bytes, in the current high-density form. Aside from holding about 20 percent more information, the 3.5-inch disks are small enough to slip into a pocket and sturdy enough to safely carry around in a pocket, purse, briefcase, or backpack or, if you have the knack, to spin across the room.

If you have the choice, get both sizes of floppy disk drives on a PC, so you can trade either size with owners of other computers. Whatever you do, don't get a PC that takes only 5.25-inch disks, which are nearly obsolete; it would be like buying a phonograph turntable rather than a CD player today.

HARD DRIVE

Inside the main box is a hard disk drive, actually a stack of platters that spin all the time, 10 times as fast as a floppy disk spins; it holds much more information, as much as box after box after box of floppy disks. The hard drive holds both the software that you run your business with and all the information that your business produces or relies on. You will never see the hard disk, even if you open the computer. It is sealed from anything that could hurt it except, like the rest of us, time and bad luck. Even the smallest hard drives hold about 20 times more than a floppy. Don't fool around with the smallest sizes, however; with your luck you'll live to regret it. Somewhere above 200 megabytes is the lowest-capacity hard disk you should consider, and twice that size is not at all extravagant. There is no such thing as a hard disk that is too big, just a hard disk that is too expensive.

If hard disks are so big and fast, why use floppies at all? First, most software you buy comes on floppies. You copy the program from the floppy disks you buy to your hard disk. Second, hard drives eventually fail, as do automobiles, hair dryers, and every living thing except you personally. If your hard disk goes bananas the day before a client expects her completed tax return or ransom note, you had better have a floppy copy. The one thing you can count on in this brave new world is that a hard disk will never fail when it doesn't much matter.

CD-ROM DRIVE

There may also be a CD-ROM drive with an entry slot on the outside of the big box. (CD stands for *compact disk*, ROM for *read-only memory*.) Into that slot you slip CD-ROMs, which are like musical CDs except that they can hold text and pictures as well as sound. The amount of information the disks hold would require something like 60 floppies or choke even the biggest hard drives. CD-ROM drives are sometimes called readers, because you can look at or listen to the information they contain, but you can't change it or add to it. If a CD-ROM drive comes with the computer, make sure it is "double speed," if not "triple speed" or "quadruple speed." You will find more information about this in Chapters 4 and 5.

There are other kinds of drives, but floppy, hard, and CD-ROMs are the most common and the only sorts you have to worry about now, and probably forever.

CHIPS

These are little fingernails of silicon graven with incredibly complex circuits that run the computer. In a photographic enlargement, a chip looks like a map of a metropolitan area, with its streets and highways, skyscrapers and housing developments, boarded-up downtown and crowded suburban malls. The main chip is named the CPU, even though the whole box is sometimes mistakenly called that.

In a PC, a Pentium is the CPU you should get, or, by now, a Sexium or whatever they finally call the 686. A 486/DX is the least CPU you should settle for. If the first number is 486, or 80486, or i486, the numbers after DX should be no lower than 2 and 66. Apple, the maker of the Macintosh, is in a major state of transition in CPUs at this writing. Our best guess is that numbers bigger than 6100/60, the least you can buy, are the least you should settle for. But it is difficult to be strongly opinionated about the Power Macs right now because they are so new. If you go for one of the older Macintoshes, 68040 is the number you want.

The other chips are for memory, also known as *RAM* because it is so macho. RAM chips remember the words and numbers and pictures you make and manipulate. When the power goes off— because you flipped the switch or a tree fell on the power line or you forgot to pay the electric bill or because, and this is very important, the utility company screws up or is overloaded for even a fraction of a second—the memory chips forget everything they ever knew. That is why the computer has disk drives: to store the data so you can load it back into the memory chips tomorrow.

Figure 1.3 The Power Macintosh® 7100/66, based on the Power PC 601 microprocessor. It is shown with the Apple display, keyboard, and mouse.

It is psychotic not to be neurotic about saving your work on a disk every so often, the more often the better. One of us saves on the hard disk whenever he stands up for any reason, and puts an extra copy on a floppy disk at the end of the day. The other one of us saves on the hard disk whenever she goes to the bathroom, and practically never on a floppy disk. (Names withheld.) If Ole or Murph down at the electric company dozes off for a minute, he doesn't lose the report you've been crafting all morning. *You* do.

WHAT IT ALL MEANS

CPU

Central Processing Unit, the chip inside the main box that does the work. PCs operate with CPUs made by Intel, for the most part, and the Pentium and 80486 are the important ones now. Macs operate with CPUs made by Motorola. The 68030 and 68040 were important the day before yesterday; PowerPC chips with a variety of numbers are important now.

RAM

Random Access Memory, where programs and information are stored when the power is on. It is random access because the CPU can go directly to where data are stored, as you change directly from channel 2 to channel 7 on a remote control instead of having to slog through channels 3, 4, 5, and 6, as you do with a rotary dial on a television set.

ROM

With RAM, you can get information (read) and store or alter (write) it. With ROM, *Read Only Memory*, you can only get information, you can't store new information or change old information. The ROM contains instructions that the computer cannot do without and that must not be changed. ROMs in Macintoshes hold more information than ROMs in PCs.

MEMORY

A lot of the computers advertised in newspapers and magazines come with four megabytes of RAM. That is not because four megabytes is enough memory. It is so the companies can put a low price in their ads. You can get by for a while with four megabytes of RAM, but eventually you'll be sorry. Get at least eight megabytes to begin with and you'll thank us in your prayers. Sixteen megabytes is even better, but it is not as much better than eight megabytes as eight megabytes is than four megabytes. If you buy a Power Mac, however, go for sixteen megabytes if you possibly can.

WHAT IT ALL MEANS

BIT

The smallest unit of data. A bit, short for *binary digit*, is usually thought of as being either a 1 or a 0, because we can do arithmetic with 1s and 0s. If we were doing logic with bits, we would think of them as "true/false." In other contexts, they might be "either/or," "yes/no," "male/female," or "Republican/Democrat." Computers reduce the whole complicated world, which is full of maybes, to "1/0."

continued...

BYTE

Eight bits. A byte stores a letter, number, or other character or command. A capital *A* is 01000001, a carriage return is 00001101. Everything in a document, even a space (00100001), is at least one byte. The business user wouldn't need to know what either a bit or a byte is if they weren't components of kilobytes and megabytes, which you will run into.

KILOBYTE

A thousand, actually 1024, bytes. A double-spaced one-page business letter takes about two kilobytes of memory or storage.

MEGABYTE

A million, actually 1,048,575, bytes. The working memory in your computer takes up four or, better, eight or, better still, sixteen megabytes. The hard disk stores 200 or more megabytes.

OVERBYTE

There are bigger combinations of bytes—a gigabyte is about a billion bytes—that you are not likely to encounter today, but may run into tomorrow.

It is often cheaper to buy extra memory when you buy the computer than to add memory later. It is always easier, because to add memory later you have to open the case and root around among the power supply and plunger and resistors and fuses, or unplug everything and take the box to the shop where a technician will put in the memory. The technician may well make more money than you do, and he is making it off you, and he is certainly making more money than you are while your computer is in the shop.

WHAT IT ALL MEANS

MOTHERBOARD

The main circuit board inside the box to which everything else is attached.

SLOTS

Spaces inside the main box in which accessory circuit boards are attached to the motherboard.

BAYS

Similar to slots, except you can get to them from the outside to insert floppy disks, CD-ROMs, tapes, and such.

MULTIMEDIA

Computers and programs that can run more than one medium at a time—not just text, but text plus sound, or text plus videos, or text plus sound and videos.

MPC

Multimedia Personal Computer. Currently MPC2 is the minimum, and we do mean minimum, standard for a PC to run multimedia.

There are many other things inside the computer, known to technological sophisticates as gizmos and gewgaws. Don't worry about them.

KEYBOARDS

Writers about such things always start with the typewriter keyboard as an analogy for the computer keyboard. The letters and numbers and punctuation marks are in the same place on both keyboards, but the computer keyboard has more keys—to do things that computers can do and typewriters can't. The trouble with the analogy is that for many younger people the computer keyboard came first, and the typewriter keyboard is a relic, like phonographs and mechanical can openers and noncable television.

Oh, well. The keys that are on a computer keyboard, and not on a typewriter keyboard, include **Enter** (sometimes called **Return** or just marked with an arrow pointed down and left), **Ctrl**, **Alt**, **Esc**, **Num Lock**, **Scroll Lock**, **Print Screen**, BS (just kidding), **F1** through **F10** or **F12** and, on the Macintosh, **Command** (with an apple or a California cloverleaf symbol or both on it), and **Option**. There are also arrow keys, which can be pressed to move the arrow on the screen instead of rolling a mouse, and a separate batch of number keys in addition to the number keys on the top row along with **!**, **@**, and **#**.

People like accountants, who spend a lot of time typing numbers, find this separate set of keys, called the *numeric keypad*, faster to touch-type on and less prone to error.

The **Enter** key is pressed to tell the computer to do something and at the end of a paragraph; the **Esc** (for Escape) key usually gets you out of something, i.e., it escapes, and most of the other special keys are pressed with another key or two to accomplish tasks that may or may not differ from one program to another.

On a PC running Windows, for instance, holding down the **Ctrl** (Control) key while pressing the **s** key usually saves a copy of whatever you are working on to the disk, as does holding down the **Command** and **s** keys on a Macintosh. On a PC, for another example, holding down the **Ctrl**, **Alt**, and **Del** (Delete) keys together restarts everything and loses any work you haven't saved on a disk. It seems like a weird combination until you realize you could never hit those three keys together accidentally. It is hard enough to hit those three keys together deliberately, and doing it is known as the "three-fingered salute." You should not make a three-fingered salute unless you must, any more than you should make a one-fingered salute unless sorely provoked.

The function keys (the ones with "F" and a number) do different things in different programs, or nothing at all, but you can usually count on the **F1** key to put a file of help on the screen of a PC running Windows or to undo the last thing you did on a Macintosh.

MOUSE

A mouse comes with all personal computers these days. You can operate a PC running Microsoft Windows without a mouse, but it is a pain in the neck, and you cannot always run all the software you want to use with it. You can't operate a Macintosh at all without a mouse. A mouse, a little box about the size and shape of a bar of soap, is moved around on the table to move the pointer on the screen. A ball on the underside of the mouse rolls when you move the creature on the tabletop, and that movement is transmitted through the tail of the mouse, a cable, to the computer itself.

A PC mouse has two or three buttons on it, although no one has ever figured out what to do with the button in the middle. A Macintosh mouse has only one button.

After you move the pointer on the screen with the mouse, you click a button once, or twice in rapid succession, or hold it down to select or start a program, mark a number, word or whole section of numbers or words to change, move, or get rid of, to draw a line, or to call Domino's Pizza.

There are also mice that are not attached directly to the computer with a cable, but communicate with it with an infrared beam, or maybe via satellite or Federal Express. If you can keep a clear line of sight between mouse and receiver, you might like one of them. We can't, and don't.

TRACKBALL

A trackball, which some folks prefer, is an upside-down mouse, with the ball on top. With a trackball, you only have to roll the ball, not the whole unit.

Some people despise both mice and trackballs, because they make them take their fingers off the keyboard and interrupt their typing. It is a good idea, though, to remove your fingers from the keyboard often. You'll find more on this in Chapter 3.

PORTABLE COMPUTERS

The preceding was written on the assumption that you will work with a desktop computer, one that ordinarily stays in place, rather than a portable computer, one that you can carry around. There are definite advantages, and clear disadvantages, to a portable computer.

ADVANTAGES

The obvious strong point is that portables weigh from less than 4 pounds to 10 or so pounds and have widths and depths ranging from the size of a sheet of typing paper on down. (Computers that fit in the palm of a hand can be helpful accessories, and are cute, but are not much good as primary machines.)

A portable—there are notebooks, subnotebooks, laptops, and other ill-defined categories—can sit on the airplane's seat tray, on the seat of a car or commuter train, on your lap at poolside or on a cruise ship, or even on a bar if you have a designated driver. It can go wherever you go, if you don't mind lugging it along. That is the big appeal, and the one that is touted in advertisements. More telling, perhaps, is that you can take a portable to a client's home or office to show work in progress, or to clinch a sale.

If your own space is tight, you can work at the kitchen or dining room table and, when meal time comes, close the computer and put it away. You can, as Larry does, write on the back porch in summer, or in front of the fireplace in winter. This book was written on a subportable PC, a Zeos Contenda, then transferred to a Macintosh Quadra 660AV for fine tuning.

And if you must keep a childproof house, it is much easier to stow away a portable.

There are portable PCs from IBM and a host of other companies, and Macintosh PowerBooks from Apple. Things are easier if both your portable and desktop machines are PCs, or if both are Macs. But one of each is an acceptable solution if you can put up with a bit more trouble in transferring files from one to the other.

Figure 1.4 The PowerBook 540c is Apple's highest performance active matrix color notebook computer.

DISADVANTAGES

That four-pound portable isn't all you carry around. There will be an accessory floppy drive if one isn't built in, adding a pound or so to the weight; a brick of an AC adapter for when the battery runs down; spare floppy disks for backups and emergencies; an accessory modem if one isn't built in; a printer cable or perhaps even a printer, a tire jack and blender and the dozens of other devices that computers pester you to buy.

And someone who wouldn't break into your house or apartment and make off with the double-digit poundage of a loaded Pentium and its 21-inch monitor might well snatch a little portable on impulse when your attention is distracted.

PORTABLE HARDWARE

This section follows the same order of categories as the part on desktop computers, and assumes you have read that.

MONITOR

The screen, about 7 to 10 inches diagonally, is an LCD (*liquid crystal display*) like the numbers on a digital watch, not a tube like a television set. If it is not backlit, it will be difficult to read for any length of time in anything but good light. Backlighting or *edgelighting* (a light behind or on the side of the screen) improve the readability in any light but good light, but drain the battery faster. There are also monochrome, gray-scale and color, and passive matrix, dual scan, and active-matrix screens, which get better and more expensive and power-hungry as you move through the list.

Most portables can be attached to a regular monitor when you're off the road.

DISK DRIVES

The hard drive is the same as in a desktop computer, only physically smaller and probably with less capacity. The 3.5-inch floppy drive may be built in, adding weight and convenience, or an accessory attached separately, lessening the immediate weight but adding to the inconvenience.

There may also be one or more slots for PCMCIA (never mind) cards, credit-card sized things that can substitute for disk drives, memory, and modems.

KEYBOARD

The keyboard may be identical in size and number of keys to a regular keyboard, which makes typing easier and carrying harder, or significantly smaller with some keys doing double duty, which makes typing harder and carrying easier.

MOUSE

The mouse, actually a trackball or trackpoint or pressure-sensitive pad, can be built in practically anywhere you can reach or not reach. None of the mouse devices in portable computers are as easy to use as a real mouse or trackball, but you can get used to them as you can get used to a nagging little pain. Of course, you can attach a real mouse to a portable, which makes it a little easier to use and a little less portable.

Finally, some portables have matching docking stations. The docking station is the part of the desktop computer that was left off or compromised on the portable. They have full-sized monitors and lots more places to plug things into. They are expensive. They are not as expensive as a second computer. They are also not as handy as a second computer.

Finally, really finally this time, portables cost more than equivalent desktop computers, have little or no room for upgrading (you can move most desktops into the next technological generation one step at a time), and are *trés* cool. If your first computer isn't a portable—we can argue both sides of that question—the second should be.

Two computers? Sure. One for the desk and one for the road. One for you and one for the helper that your increasingly successful business calls for. One for you to work on and one for the kids to play games on. Or one for you to work on and one for you to play games on.

Of course, the computers will be connected in a *network*. That means, for one example, that the second computer, a portable with a little hard drive, can run programs and deal with information on the first computer, a desktop with a big hard drive. Networking two or more computers can be easy or hard. Easy if they're Macintoshes, hard if they're PCs.

Macintoshes have the software and hardware for a simple network, AppleTalk, built in. You buy the cables to attach the computers, printers, modems, or whatever together, and follow the directions in the manual that came with the computer.

PCs don't have the software and hardware built in, unless you deliberately buy them that way in the first place. Even then, connecting them in a network is a job for someone else to do. There is also specialized software (Traveling Software's LapLink) that offers some of the advantages of a network without setting one up.

PRINTERS

Some day, we have been told for years, we will have the paperless office. And someday we will have the foodless kitchen, the competent Congress, and intelligent television. In the meantime, you need a printer.

LASER PRINTERS

The printer you need is a laser printer. (There are also LED printers, which amount to the same thing except for where the light comes from.) It works much the same way as a copying machine works, and everybody knows you can use a copying machine or drive a car or watch a television set without knowing how they work.

What is important is the printer's *resolution* and speed. Resolution is measured in dots per inch (dpi), and the more dots per inch the sharper the letters and numbers look. The first laser printers produced 300 dots per inch, and that looked great until printers producing 400 dots per inch came along, and that looked greater still until printers producing 600 dots per inch came along. (The machine in a professional print shop may produce a couple of thousand dots per inch.)

Figure 1.5 The HP LaserJet 4L printer is Hewlett-Packard Company's lowest priced personal laser printer. The 4ppm, 300dpi printer includes an easy one-button control panel, and software for automatic printer setup.

Speed is measured in pages per minute (ppm). A low-end laser printer for undemanding tasks turns out four pages per minute. If you do a lot of printing, or if you print long documents, go for six or eight pages per minute. The ppm rating comes from the manufacturer. If you print the same page over and over again, and there are no changes of typefaces or pictures, and you make a human sacrifice, you will get close to the rated speed, just as you will get 38 miles a gallon if you drive a perfectly tuned car at the optimum speed on a level highway at 3 in the morning.

WHAT IT ALL MEANS

HPPCL AND POSTSCRIPT

Laser printers speak one of two main languages: HPPCL, the Hewlett-Packard Printer Control Language, or PostScript. An HPPCL-speaking printer is fine for most purposes. People who publish a lot of fancy stuff should spring for the extra cost of a PostScript-literate printer. Also at extra cost, many non-PostScript printers can "emulate"—pretend they are—PostScript printers.

INKJET PRINTERS

These spray the dots of ink on the page through tiny holes. The printed output is almost as good-looking as what comes from laser printers, but not quite, and the machines are usually slower and cheaper, although not necessarily cheaper to operate. They will do if you can't afford a laser printer.

DOT-MATRIX PRINTERS

These pound the dots on the page through an inked ribbon. Some are very noisy, and others are merely noisy, and the printed output is either very bad or merely bad. Aside from being a little cheaper than inkjet printers, and a lot cheaper than laser printers, they have one advantage: they can turn out copies on multipart forms. If you must produce copies routinely, get a dot-matrix printer. If you don't produce copies routinely, avoid them.

The ideal compromise, which costs only money and space, is to buy two printers: a dot-matrix for copies, in-house memos and notes and maybe for strictly personal correspondence; a laser or inkjet printer for the working stuff. There is no surer sign to outsiders that you are working in your home, on a tight budget, than documents that come out of a dot-matrix printer. Even people who don't understand the technology will know that something is wrong.

That reminds us of another matter. With a laser printer, and the right software and paper stock, you can create your own business cards and letterheads. It is perfectly all right to print them too, but get both of them done by a professional print shop if you can afford it. Handsome as they can be, the homemade versions carry the same subtle message as dot-matrix printouts.

Whatever you do, don't yield to the temptation to skimp on the printer. Clients don't see you struggling with an old computer or a slow modem. They judge you by the printouts.

OTHER PRINTERS

There are also daisy-wheel and thermal printers, which are obsolete, though you may still run into them. Avoid them like the plague, to coin a phrase. There are portable printers that can go on trips to keep your portable computer company, or fit into a tiny home office, but they lack many of the features of full-sized printers. Don't get one unless you absolutely need one. There are special printers for such special purposes as turning out labels. But you can print labels on your regular printer once you set it up to do that.

COLOR PRINTERS

A dash of color adds more than a dash of interest to a letter or flyer. You don't want a color dot-matrix printer, and you can't afford a color laser printer. A color inkjet printer is approachable, but make sure you like its output before you buy it. Especially, make sure you like its black-and-white output before you buy it. And don't expect anything to look like a page from National Geographic. Remember: A dash of color, not the ceiling of the Sistine Chapel. Color printers are improving in quality and price practically weekly, but it is easy to fool yourself about how good they really are.

THREE-IN-ONE EQUIPMENT

Besides a computer, the home office certainly needs a printer, and probably a fax and a copier. They cost money, take up room, and require three electrical plugs. Suppose you could put them all in one box, like a microwave oven that could also open cans and pull corks out of wine bottles? At least two companies have.

The Panasonic PFC (Printer Fax Copier) occupies about the same amount of desk space as a sheet of typing paper—that's called its footprint—and costs somewhat less than the three separate machines would. The printer is described in ads as "laser quality," (that means ink-jet, a forgivable exaggeration), prints four pages a minute at 300 dots per inch. That also describes the copier. And plugged into the telephone line, the PFC can send and receive faxes. The faxes you get are on good paper, not that creepy thermal stuff affordable faxes use.

The Hewlett-Packard Office Jet offers similar features, plus the enviable H-P reputation.

So why not buy one?

To begin with, you have to buy all three(-in-one) at the same time. In the normal course of home-office events, you buy, say, a printer, and after a few months of squirreling quarters (well, dollars) away you buy a fax machine, and then relatives pool their money together and give you a copier for your birthday. That's the way many home offices get equipped, in stages, as money and opportunity present themselves.

Figure 1.6 Buying three pieces of equipment in one package can be like having a pet bunnyroosaurus. It may be powerful but the parts don't always work as well as they might.

Second, a fax machine will serve as a copier, even if it does use thermal paper, until you get a real one. That's why the best order of purchase is 1) printer, 2) fax, and 3) copier. Indeed, if your computer has a fax modem, and it should, that will serve for a while too. Come to think of it, a scanner might be a better buy than a fax machine, because you can turn paper documents into files a fax modem can send, and find many other ways to use the scanner as well.

Third, despite the handiness of the multipurpose machine, none of its components, particularly the printer, are as good as the best standalone devices. You really should have a laser printer. If you've planned to save money in that category by buying an ink-jet printer, you probably can't afford a three-in-one anyway.

Finally, and most importantly, machines break. They have to be taken to the shop, left there until next Friday (which means the following Wednesday), and then picked up. You would hate to lose your printer for a week, or your fax, or your copier. How about losing all three when only one is broken? When you were the second Assistant Vice President of post-planning at the Xeroid Corporation and the printer went down, you used another printer on the network, or walked down the hall to the unaccounting department with a floppy disk in hand. At home, we don't have two printers, and neither do you. And if the broken component can't be repaired, at least economically, you have to replace all three even if two are in fine shape.

MODEMS

Modems let your computer communicate with other computers through phone lines. That sounds like recreation for your computer, rather than something you want to do. But modems can gather vast amounts of information without making you leave your desk, let you talk with other people in your own or related fields, and promote, though not really advertise, your services. There will be more on this in Chapters 4 and 5. But most modems can also be used as fax machines, so they have to be mentioned now.

Almost certainly there is, or will be, a fax machine in your home office, so clients can communicate with you, and so you can communicate with them or order a B.L.T. and coffee from the deli. Fax machines are great inventions, more immediately and obviously useful than computers themselves, and really unreplaceable; if you need one at all you can't do without one. However, most modems will also double as fax machines, much as most fax machines will also double as copiers. That is, you can prepare a letter or report or spreadsheet or drawing or whatever you prepare for money on your computer and send it directly from there to a fax machine, or to another computer with a fax modem, without printing it out. And it will look better when received than it would if it were sent by regular fax.

You can also receive a document from a fax machine, or fax modem, on your computer and print it out only if you need a paper copy. If you do print it out, by the way, it won't be on that slick, curly, short-lived fax paper.

A fax modem is not a complete substitute for a real fax machine— you can't scrawl a note or a drawing on it at the last minute—but it is a worthy accessory, and it can be a stand-alone substitute in a pinch.

Make sure the modem can both send and receive faxes. The early ones could only send them, and the manufacturer or dealer may be trying to palm off unsold inventory on unsuspecting customers.

The single greatest danger posed by computers is not cramped wrists (see Chapter 3 for more about wrists) but that you might get more interested in your computer equipment than in the real estate or kennel or ticket-scalping business, or whatever your racket is.

REMINDER LIST: BUYING GUIDE

- **Monitor.** In a desktop, about 14 inches, VGA or SVGA, 256 colors, or gray scale. The monitor works in conjunction with a circuit card (board) in the computer; the card should be capable of generating the highest resolutions and greatest number of colors, or grays, the monitor is capable of. In a portable, whatever you can afford and live with.

- **Main Box.** Pentium or 486/DX/66 (PC), 68040 (regular Macintosh), better than 6100 (Power Mac), 3.5-inch high-density floppy drive, 200-plus-megabyte hard drive, eight or sixteen megabytes of RAM, at least a double-speed CD-ROM drive.

- **Keyboard.** Ideally, you should try out a keyboard before you buy it, but no store is going to let you spend enough time with one to really get a feel for it.

- **Mouse or Trackball.** Whichever you like best.

- **Printer.** First choice, a laser printer. Second choice, an inkjet printer. Fifth choice, a dot-matrix printer, unless you must print multipart forms.

- **Modem.** One capable of both sending and receiving faxes. At least 14.4 in speed (details in Chapter 4).

2

THE SOFT PART

TO DO LIST

- ✓ Operating systems
- ✓ Integrated programs
- ✓ Word processors
- ✓ Spreadsheets
- ✓ Databases
- ✓ Graphics
- ✓ Communications
- ✓ Printer drivers

The hardware you've lavished so much time, attention, and money on can hardly do a blessed thing. When you turn on a PC or Macintosh it checks itself out for a few seconds, and then it looks for instructions. The instructions are in the *operating system*—DOS, with Microsoft Windows on top of it in the case of a PC; the System, with the Finder on top of it in the case of a Mac.

Not until the operating system is loaded into the computer's memory does that expensive wonder of the age know what to do when you press a key, move a mouse, save a file onto a disk or, for that matter, try to get a file from a disk. The operating system is software, the program or collection of programs containing the instructions the computer needs to act like a computer at all. And every other program is also a set of instructions.

Even if a printer is hooked up correctly to the computer, it won't print diddly without a program that tells it how to do what it was built to do. The same goes for the modem, the mouse, everything. Some of this essential software comes with the operating system as the operating system usually comes with the computer, some comes with peripherals like printers and modems, and some you have to buy separately.

OPERATING SYSTEMS

Without an operating system, you can't do anything. With an operating system, you can't do anything anyone will pay you for without further software. But the operating system comes first. This book assumes your computer runs either Microsoft Windows 3.1 and DOS 6.2 as the operating system for a PC, or System 7.1 on a Macintosh. There are other possibilities, and most of the book will still be useful if your computer marches to a different drummer, but the ones assumed here are the most common and, for non-nerds, the least intimidating. (Windows 4.0 was in gestation and System 7.5 was being born during this writing.)

MICROSOFT WINDOWS

To be brutally frank about it, Windows turns a PC into an imitation Macintosh. The first version of Windows turned a PC into an impoverished imitation of a Macintosh.

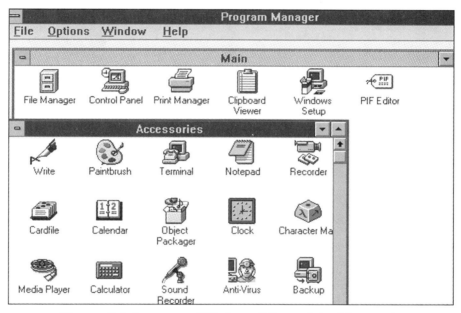

Figure 2.1 Icons turn PCs into siblings of the Macintosh.

The second Windows version turned a PC into a poor imitation of a Mac, but above the poverty level. The third Windows, 3.0, and its successor, 3.1, turned a PC into a pretty good imitation of a Mac, like a brother who makes $50,000 a year against his twin's $70,000. Windows 4.0 should put them about neck and neck.

The underlying command system behind Windows (up to version 3.1) is DOS, a cryptic Disk Operating System that demands the typing of difficult-to-remember and unforgiving commands like:

```
"copy c:\dearmom.ltr a:\dearpop.ltr"
```

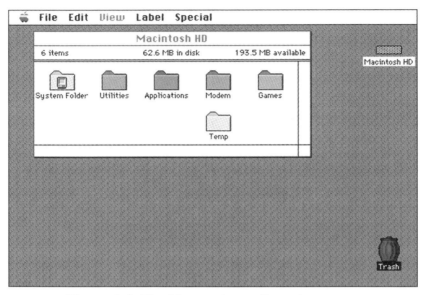

Figure 2.2 The Macintosh is still simpler to use.

Windows requires pointing an arrow at a picture or word and clicking a button on a mouse, except when you have to type a DOS, or DOS-like command, which you sometimes have to do anyway. Windows, like the Mac System, is supposed to make running a computer "intuitive," as if the random forces of evolution or God on the sixth day built into humans the instinctive capability of handling a Graphical User Interface. Well, maybe.

THE MACINTOSH SYSTEM

To operate a Mac, you point the arrow and click.

WHAT IT ALL MEANS

VERSION NUMBERS

The first issue of a program is 1.0; the second issue, with a major change, is 2.0. Between 1.0 and 2.0 will be versions with small improvements and small, or not so small, corrections, numbered 1.01 or 1.2 or 1.23. The smart money never buys a version that ends with ".0." The version that ends with ".1" or higher has the worst errors of ".0" fixed. Maybe.

GUI

Pronounced "gooey," this stands for *Graphical User Interface*. It means you do things with little drawings called icons, rather than with words. Microsoft Windows and the Macintosh System are both GUIs.

BUYING SOFTWARE

Even if you don't know much about software, you know how to run your business. If you write letters and reports, you need a word-processing program. If you keep track of numbers and do arithmetic with them, you need a spreadsheet program. If you handle lists of information like the names and addresses of clients, you need a database program. If you print any of this stuff out (and who doesn't?), you need a printer driver (a driver is a little program that operates—drives—a device attached to the computer). If you communicate with other computers over telephone lines, you need a communications program. If you show clients compelling presentations on the screen, or in printed copies, you need a presentation or publication program, or both. Probably you do two or more of these things. Then you have to buy two or more separate programs. Unless you buy one program that can do more than one thing.

This chapter is about the basic kinds of software. There is more about software in Chapter 5 and how and where to buy it in Chapter 6.

INTEGRATED PROGRAMS

Software that can do several things is an integrated program. An integrated program cannot do any one of the things that it does as well as a program designed just to do one thing well, but it may do all or most of them well enough.

The two leaders of integrated software are Microsoft Works and ClarisWorks, with versions for both PCs and Macs, followed by PFS:WindowWorks. With them, you can write, juggle numbers and names, add graphics to your documents and print them out, and communicate with other computers. At any given moment, Microsoft Works is ahead of ClarisWorks; at the next given moment, ClarisWorks is ahead of Microsoft Works. "Ahead of" means doing more things or doing them better, and the publishers are forever bringing out updated versions of the programs.

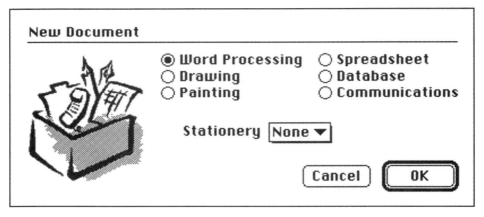

Figure 2.3 One set of commands works for all Works programs.

Pick wisely, because once you get accustomed to one program and have entered a vast amount of information in it, it is a time-consuming chore to switch to the other. How do you pick wisely? If there is one special task that is essential to your business—alphabetizing customer's names backward, say, or selecting the winner of the seventh race at Hialeah—see if one program can do it and the other can't. Otherwise, flip a coin. (You may not have to flip a coin. The price of a new computer often includes one of the integrated programs, or still another, which will probably have "Works" in its name.)

Another tip that fits in here: People who are fascinated by computers and their programs love to discover new software from obscure companies that can do new things, or can do old things better. People who are trying to make a living stick with the leaders. Stick with the leaders.

An integrated program is a good way to get started with a computer, and you may use it forever. The other possibility is that one component of the program won't have all the features you need, but the rest will do fine. An accountant or other heavy number juggler, for instance, may need an industrial-strength spreadsheet, although the word-processing and communications modules of Whatever Works are okay otherwise. A writer may need a major word processor, a salesman may need a powerful database manager, a pornographer a sexy presentation program. All these specialists may use one or two specialized programs, and rely on the integrated program for everything else.

Software publishers also bundle all their top programs in specially-priced packages called *suites*. That means you get a major word processor, spreadsheet, and whatever, three to five programs altogether for considerably less than they would cost if you bought them separately. If several other people work for you, and they do a variety of things, a suite may be the way to go. If you do all or most of the work yourself, however, it is highly unlikely that you will learn all of the major features and a bunch of the minor features of WordPerfect, Lotus 1-2-3, dBASE, and ProComm, and still get all or most of the work done. Also remember, publishers frequently update their programs to correct errors, add features, and make more money. Are you really going to keep four or five programs up-to-date?

With portable computers, integrated programs are definitely the way to go. Portables usually have smaller hard disks than desktops and integrated programs take up less room than the equivalent number of full-featured programs. If you do only one thing with a portable, perhaps write, you can spare the space for a big-name word processor. But if you do two or three things with a portable, say write, keep a spreadsheet and consult a name-and-address listing, an integrated program will require a lot less room than three separate major programs.

Now to the major categories of non-integrated (segregated?) programs.

WORD PROCESSORS

More people use these than any other category of software. You may be running a business where you never write a letter, proposal, or report, but we doubt it. With a word processor, you can write, correct, and pretty up the page before you make a printed copy. Most of the programs can also check your spelling and grammar, find a synonym for a word you've employed too much, and let you try out different typefaces and styles. When the copy comes out of the printer it will be perfect. Sure. At least when you spot an error or room for improvement in the printed copy, you can easily fix it up on the computer and print it out again.

Windows comes with a simple word processor called Write, good enough for letters, and the Macintosh system comes with an even simpler word processor, TeachText. Windows also has Notepad (one word), and the Mac has Note Pad (two words), both good enough for memos to yourself and to-do lists.

The leading stand-alone word-processing programs are Microsoft Word and WordPerfect, with both Windows and Macintosh versions, and Ami Pro, for Windows only. There are several followers. Claris MacWrite Pro, for one, is very nice for the Macintosh, as is WriteNow, for two, and Q&A Write and Professional Write for Windows and DOS PCs.

Jan writes with WordPerfect on her Windows PC and can't abide anything else. Larry vacillates between Professional Write and ClarisWorks on the PC and ClarisWorks and WordPerfect on the Macintosh. ClarisWorks is fine for newspaper articles, which are generally short and are sent from Larry's little computer to the newspaper's big computer as plain text, without any fancy formatting. Since it is an integrated program, ClarisWorks also lets him keep his name-and-address database and, when he remembers to use it, expenses spreadsheet, a few mouse strokes away. This book was written with Professional Write, a fast and lean-featured program, on a portable PC, and then transferred to a Macintosh running WordPerfect for formatting.

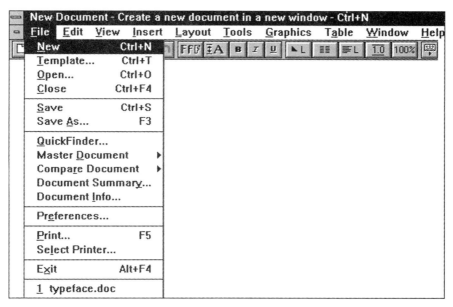

Figure 2.4 Write, edit, proofread, and doodle, all with your word processor.

It may border on heresy to say this, but with modern PC's and Macs it doesn't make that much difference which of the major word-processing programs you buy, unless one of them offers a particular feature you need and the others don't. If you absolutely must produce Cyrillic footnotes, ask the salesperson or read the back of the box, and don't fully believe either one of them. The phone number of the publisher should be somewhere on the package, or you can get it from the salesperson or from an ad in a computer magazine (you don't have to actually read the wretched thing). You can probably believe the publishing company, if you can reach a human being there by phone, which is doubtful.

By the way, if you have a typewriter, don't throw it away. Firing up a computer and printer, and starting a word-processing program can be annoying in the extreme when you just want to type a few sentences or address an envelope. You could also write with a pencil or pen if you remember how to do that.

SPREADSHEETS

Spreadsheets are to numbers what word processors are to words. The computerized spreadsheet brought personal computers into the office, not the computerized typewriter. After all, word processing made typing documents much easier and more efficient, but in the office of the late '70s and early '80s, most typing was done by women. Spreadsheets were men's work, like hunting and fishing. Typing was sewing and frying the fish.

Spreadsheets are made up of columns, which go up and down and are labeled with letters, and rows, which go from side to side and are labeled with numbers. A cell, the rectangle where columns and rows meet (say C3 or P12 or SS163), holds a name like *Accounts Receivable*, or a number like *12509*, or a formula like *C3+P12*9* to do arithmetic with one or a bunch of numbers.

	File Edit Format Arrange Options View					
			TERI'S TUTORING EXPENSES (SS)			
	A	**B**	**C**	**D**	**E**	**F**	**G**
1		SEPT	OCT	NOV	DEC	JAN	TOTAL
2	BOOKS	125.98	0	0	0	98.55	224.53
3	PAPER	23.78	0	23.78	0	23.78	71.34
4	ASPIRIN	1.11	2.22	3.33	4.44	555.55	566.65
5	COMP. DISKS	25.67	0	0	0	25.67	51.34
6	TELEPHONE	23.76	31.21	21.21	26.87	27.04	130.09
7	PROMOTION	56.65	0	0	0	0	56.65
8	BRIBES	123.45	0	0	45.43	211.11	379.99
9							
10	TOTAL	380.4	33.43	48.32	76.74	941.7	1480.59

Figure 2.5 Spreadsheets save the headaches of recalculating every time you change a number.

You can put your budget in a spreadsheet, or your expenses, or your best guesses as to what a job will cost, and the computer will do the arithmetic. Working out a good spreadsheet model is not an easy task, any more than writing a good business letter is easy, but once you've done it you can play with it...er, work with it...endlessly. The January telephone bill comes in; you enter the total into its cell in the spreadsheet, and all the other numbers in the spreadsheet that are affected by the telephone bill change in an instant—or two. Or you can really play with it. What would happen to a year's expenses if you bought paper clips by the case instead of the box and sent letters by the Postal Service instead of Federal Express? Enter the new "what if" numbers and see the results. Then try again, cheating a little this time.

Top spreadsheets for PCs are Microsoft Excel, Borland Quattro Pro, and Lotus 1-2-3, and for Macs are Microsoft Excel and Lotus 1-2-3.

DATABASES

Actually called database managers, these programs manage databases. What else? A *database* is a collection of information. The phone book is a database. The difference between a printed database, like the phone book, and a software database manager is that you can look up the information in all kinds of ways. With the phone book, you look up a person's phone number or address by looking up his name, which you have to know. With a software phone book, say the list of your clients, you can also look up the information by name. Or you can look it up by address or phone number or hair color if you typed in hair color in the first place. You can also get the names of all the customers on a particular street, or with a particular area code, or in a particular zip code, or just the ones who owe you money, or just the ones whose last order was more than $50, or just the ones who haven't called in six months, or...you get the idea.

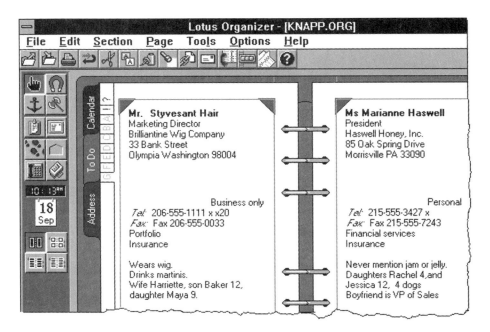

Figure 2.6 With a well-constructed database, you will never lose track of your clients.

You have to enter all the information first, which is a lot of trouble, but the more you enter, the more ways you have of categorizing the people. We're using this high-level phone book as an easy-to-understand example, but a database manager can handle any kind of information that lends itself to being listed.

Top database managers include Q&A, Claris FileMaker Pro, Lotus Approach, Borland Paradox, and Microsoft Access for the PC and lonely FileMaker Pro for the Macintosh. Usually you work out the form into which you enter information for yourself—you know what you need better than Bill Gates or Philippe Kahn—but the programs include *templates*, model forms that you can adopt as is or edit.

There are also companies that sell templates. If you belong to a professional organization for people in your line of work you can find out about them.

If your database needs are extremely simple, your regular word processor or spreadsheet can substitute. After all, you can type lists with a word processor or spreadsheet, and search for names, zip codes, and so on. But a real database manager is better.

WHAT IT ALL MEANS

FLAT FILE DATABASE

A database manager that stores its information in one table. In a client list, the blanks that you fill in with a name, address, and other information are called *fields*, and all the fields for that client are in one record in one table.

RELATIONAL DATABASE

A database manager that stores its information in several tables. In that client list, the information blanks could be in several different tables. Relational databases are more flexible than flat-file databases, as well as more expensive and often more difficult to use.

GRAPHICS PROGRAMS

This section is not about the programs used by professional graphic artists and desktop publishers. If you are one of those people, you already know about Adobe Photoshop or Aldus PageMaker or will have to find out about them somewhere else. But people who are professional accountants or consultants (whatever that is) occasionally must produce a report that looks better than what first comes out of the printer, or design an ad or flyer. Or present a proposal to a client that looks as if it was done by someone who knew what he was doing. Appearance counts, you know. A lawyer in a pin-striped suit and power tie looks like he knows a tort from a tart. You wouldn't hire an artist in a suit and tie or a business-plan advisor in torn blue jeans and worn sneakers.

You may not need a graphics program. Both Microsoft Windows and the Macintosh System come with TrueType fonts built in. If you want to print something in a type other than the one you use for letters to laggard bill-payers (**Futura bold italic**), you may already have a suitable typeface in the computer. The word-processing program you already use may have added more typefaces and styles to your computer. (This Macintosh Quadra 660AV, to which we have never deliberately added typefaces but only programs that included them, has 37 in the WordPerfect Font menu alone from smallish—9 point—to biggish—72 point.)

WHAT IT ALL MEANS

FONT

In traditional typography, a font is a given name, size, and style of type. Times Roman, 24-point, bold is one font; Times Roman, 12-point, bold is a different font, as is Times Roman, 12-point, condensed. In computerized typography, the definition of a font often does not include its size.

POINT

The unit of size of a font. A point is about one-seventy-second of an inch, so a font an inch tall is 72 points.

BIT-MAPPED FONTS

Characters drawn in a pattern of dots. Bit-mapped Times Roman, 24-point, bold is one drawing and Times Roman, 12-point, bold is another drawing. Bit-mapped fonts adhere to the traditional definition of "font." (They can be changed in limited and mostly ugly ways.)

SCALABLE FONTS

Also called *outline* fonts, these are characters described by mathematical formulas rather than locked into bit maps. Their size can be changed on the fly.

This is not a treatise on typography, on which there are many books and which merits years of study, but let us mention a few simple rules that will keep you from going astray and producing what the in-crowd calls ransom notes.

- Don't mix up a lot of type styles, like one word underlined, another *italicized*, another in **bold** type, and so on. In fact, don't underline words at all; it's left over from the middle typewriter ages, when it substituted for italic type.
- Never use more than two typefaces in one document.
- Choose two typefaces and stick with them for everything you do for a cohesive look to all your work.

This is a standard Roman typeface.

This is a bold Roman typeface.

This is a Roman italic.

This is a sans serif typeface.

This is a sans serif bold.

This is a sans serif italic.

This is specialty type. Use it sparingly.

This is script. Use it rarely. It is hard to read.

Your word processor probably goes beyond offering different faces and styles of type. There may well be options for putting in rules, arranging type in multiple columns, bringing in charts and other graphical elements.

With WordPerfect 6.0 for Windows, as one example, you can draw shapes like squares and circles, create up to six different kinds of charts, and even put video and sound clips into a document. ClarisWorks 3.0 for the Macintosh, as another example, has both drawing and painting modules to jazz up your documents. Windows also has an adequate graphics program, Paint, built in; the Macintosh doesn't.

WHAT IT ALL MEANS

DRAW PROGRAM

A graphics program that stores the pieces of a drawing as mathematical formulas. See also scalable fonts.

PAINT PROGRAM

A graphics program that stores the pieces of a drawing as bits. See also bit-mapped fonts.

With these facilities, and the similar ones in most other high-level word processors, you can brighten up a letter to a customer so much that you spend a day doing what used to take 15 or 20 minutes. For no particularly good reason, though, a professional-looking presentation from one consultant is more impressive than a bare-bones presentation from another consultant, even when their consulting skills are equal.

Spreadsheets and databases also offer graphical options. You can turn your numbers into pie charts, bar charts, all kinds of charts. Most even offer elemental word processing. It would be an interesting experiment to see how far you could go with one major program, if you had the time and inclination for experiments. Oh, yes, graphics programs.

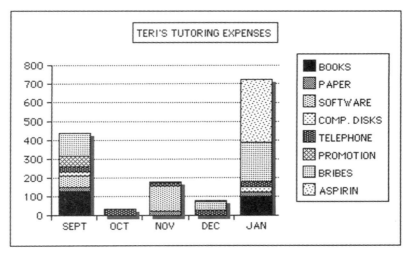

Figure 2.7 Turn anything from your database into a lively chart.

Suppose you want to go beyond your usual programs, as you probably do. The Print Shop has been popular in various forms practically since personal computers have been around, and it is available for any machine you are likely to have.

If you occasionally need to produce a greeting card, sign, banner, letterhead or calendar, it will do a good job. And if you don't use it again for a month, you won't forget how to do things. Be warned, however: It is geared toward younger users, and it is easy to turn out juvenile-looking printouts. But don't reject it out of hand. It is capable of nice work, it has a lot of accessory disks with extra graphics, fancy borders, and typefaces, and it is inexpensive.

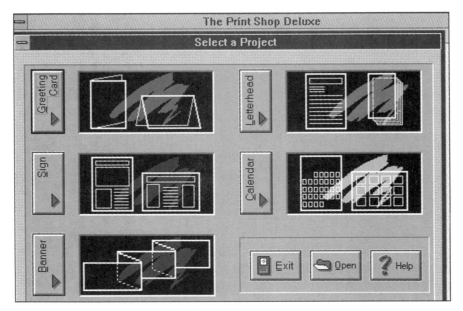

Figure 2.8 The Print Shop is not just for the kids any more.

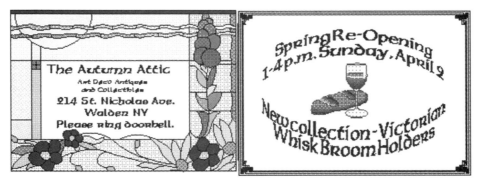

Figure 2.9 Print up a Print Shop invitation, then sit back and wait
for the customers.

MicroLogic PrintMaster Gold is similar to Print Shop, and better in
several ways, especially the CD-ROM version.

Going further along, Microsoft Publisher (for Microsoft Windows,
of course) leads you step by step through the creation of a banner,

business card and paper, calendar, envelope, flyer, greeting card and invitation, newsletter, origami, a paper airplane, and one or more of seven business forms. You may not have a use for origami or paper airplanes, but the seven business forms may be all you ever need: the customer refund, expense report, fax sheet, invoice, purchase order, statement, and quote can quickly be tailored for your business.

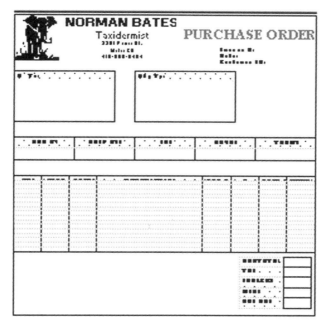

Figure 2.10 A Microsoft Publisher business form adapted by Mr. Bates.

If your needs are broader, or ambitions larger, you can call up a blank page and design a publication from scratch. There are tools galore in Microsoft Publisher for text and graphics, tables and pictures. The final product can come out of your own printer, or be put on a floppy disk and delivered to a professional service bureau. We used Microsoft Publisher for several illustrations in this book.

A bonus for some businesspeople is that the forms can be in any of 11 languages. A perky PageWizard (one of us hates "perky" things) guides you with options and suggestions.

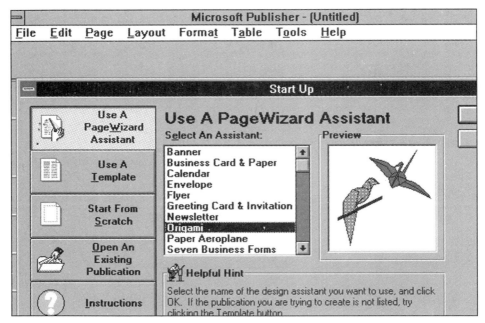

Figure 2.11 And the other thinks that "perky" can sometimes be useful.

Harvard Graphics for Windows is a leading presentation program for creating "slide" shows that can be printed out or, perhaps more effectively, shown on the computer screen. On the screen, rather than on paper, a show can incorporate such special effects as fades and wipes as well as voice and music.

There are many other presentation and publication programs—Aldus FreeHand and Microsoft PowerPoint for presentations, and Publish It! and PFS:Publisher among the other kind—but discussing them here would take us too far afield. Presumably the work you do is the main thing. But don't fail to present it well.

COMMUNICATIONS PROGRAMS

The modem you bought (a fax modem, we hope) was probably bundled with software to run it and, besides, Windows has primitive communications built in, as do many word-processing and integrated programs. If you need more flexibility, and headaches, than came with the modem, White Knight and SitComm for the Mac, ProComm Plus for the PC, and Crosstalk for both, are favorites.

The modem probably also included software for free trials of one or more of the major on-line services—CompuServe, America On-Line, Prodigy, Genie, Delphi, Tinker, Evers, and Chance. Unless you become addicted to on-line living, and it happens, one service plus the communications software will do. There is more about on-line services in Chapter 7.

PRINTER PROGRAMS

Called "drivers," they are built into Windows for any printer you are apt to use with a Windows-equipped computer, and into the Macintosh System for any printer you are apt to use with a Macintosh as long as it has Apple's name on it. Non-Apple printers made for pro-Apple Macs should come with a driver. It never hurts to ask.

Those are the major kinds of software for an office, home or otherwise. Other categories of software are dealt with in Chapter 5.

REMINDER LIST:
SOFTWARE BUYER'S GUIDE

- **Operating systems.** For a PC, Windows 3.1 and DOS 6.2. For a Macintosh, System 7.1. Better operating systems are in the wings, but don't rush in.

- **Integrated programs.** The best choice for someone with a variety of tasks, even if a major stand-alone program has to be added for one key activity.

- **Word processors.** For people with a lot of writing to do.

- **Spreadsheets.** To juggle numbers.

- **Database managers.** To make smart lists.

- **Graphics programs.** For presenting information on the printed page or the computer screen.

- **Communications programs.** So the home-office computer can talk to other computers, and send and receive faxes.

- **Printer drivers.** So the printer prints.

GETTING ORGANIZED

TO DO LIST

WHEN THERE'S NO SICK PAY

- ✓ Repetitive-stress injuries
- ✓ Eyestrain, neck- and backache
- ✓ Fertility

THE DESK AND THE ROOM

- ✓ The desk itself
- ✓ The printer stand
- ✓ The other stuff
- ✓ Electricity
- ✓ Heat and cold

THE COMPLEAT DISK

- ✓ Floppy disks
- ✓ Hard disks
- ✓ Macintosh
- ✓ Microsoft Windows
- ✓ Security

So you've got this wonderful computer system ready to run and that time-saving and energy-sparing software primed to go. Not so fast. Where are you going to put them? How are you going to feed and shelter them? How are you going to organize them and what you produce on them?

You may already have a home office—an impressive and possibly tax-deductible synonym for the place at home where you work for money instead of for the sheer joy of mowing the lawn or washing the dishes or ironing the shirts. It may be a corner of the den or dining room, even the whole of a spare bedroom that occasionally must be tidied up for an errant in-law or even a welcome guest. If it is a room that is a dedicated home office, seldom or never used as anything else, we hope it's not in the attic or basement. Neither are really suited for a computerized office. More about that later. First, though, a warning.

ON-THE-JOB INJURIES

Work-related injuries used to be associated with tough physical jobs. Carpenters smashed their fingers, telephone linemen fell off poles, firemen inhaled smoke, the removers of chicken feathers got plucked themselves. But now we know that office workers can suffer from injuries, too. (Let us not be so cynical as to suggest that such injuries only became part of the agenda when journalists began experiencing them.)

If you don't spend much time at the keyboard, if your working day involves sessions on the telephone, pacing back and forth, traveling to meet clients and prospects, you will probably be all right. Depending on how you work, the following discussion may be of minor importance or contain vital information. But workers in home offices tend to put in more time on the job than workers in regular offices. So skim this, if you must, but don't skip it.

REPETITIVE-STRESS INJURIES

The most common kinds of office injuries are *repetitive-stress injuries* or RSIs, also called *cumulative-trauma disorders*, or CTDs. They really aren't much different from tennis elbow, which thankfully is not called TE. It simply means you do the same thing over and over again, such as type, until you hurt. With typewriters, breaks were built in—returning the carriage at the end of every line, changing the paper at the end of every page. With computers, you can type all day without physical relief.

If you do spend much time at the keyboard, adjust the height of your chair and/or the height of the keyboard so that your arms are parallel to the floor and your wrists are not bent. Office-supply and computer shops sell padded wrist rests to support those old joints, or you can just roll up a towel and put it on the desk between the keyboard and the edge of the table. Splints that keep the wrists stiff may also help, especially for mouse-intensive tasks, or they may seem too psychologically orthopedic.

Several companies, Microsoft and Apple among them, offer funny-looking keyboards that may reduce strain, although no one can say for sure that they do. In any case, take breaks: go to the household equivalent of the water cooler and gossip with yourself.

You don't have to spend a lot of time fretting about RSI; do things right in the first place. But please take it seriously. Friends of ours have suffered long-term and even permanent injuries, serious enough to change their lives for the worse, from doing nothing more physically taxing than typingtypingtyping.

EYESTRAIN AND NECKACHES

RSI aside, and we hope it is, another problem in your office is the height of the monitor, the thing you stare into perhaps for hours at a time. If the monitor sits on top of the system's main box, it may be too high. Ideally, you should look straight ahead, or slightly below straight ahead, not up at all or too far down. The monitor should be about 18 to 28 inches from your eyes; you can always work with a larger size of type on the screen and reduce it before you print the document.

Here, too, no one knows for sure whether color or black-and-white displays are easier on the eyes. Probably it differs from one person to another. There is little doubt, however, that glare on the screen from a window or badly placed light fixture is not good for anyone's eyes. You can't move the window, and you may not be able to move the monitor, but you can always pull the shade, shut the blinds, or close the drapes.

NAGGING BACKACHE

In a home office, as opposed to a regular office, you have to worry about stabbing yourself in the back rather than someone else doing it for you. Your chair should not be an old dining-room chair. It should be adjustable and, especially, should support your lower back. A secretary's office chair may do, or you may have to spring for a more expensive "executive" chair. After all, if it's your business, you are an executive. Don't be tempted by one of those infinitely adjustable super recliners, however. You don't want to sprawl all over the place.

COMPUTERS AND FERTILITY

This is the dirty part. The monitor gives off radiation, and acronyms. The acronyms are VLF, Very Low Frequency, and ELF, Extremely Low Frequency, and they can hurt you. Or maybe they can't hurt you, depending on which studies you read in the paper. Don't sit close to the monitor, and especially don't sit close to the sides or back of a monitor when it is on, because more of the maybe bad or maybe not bad radiation comes from the sides and the back than from the front. Pregnant women should pay special attention to this, and everybody should consider buying a monitor that meets higher standards of radiation control, bearing in mind that no one really knows what the standards should be.

DESK ORGANIZATION

THE DESK

You have a desk, of course, or a table that does double-duty as a desk. If a full-size computer sits on top of it, there might not be enough room left for the other things that we must still keep on a desk. Paper and pencils have not gone out of style, or paper clips, or letter openers, or scissors, or a spot for a coffee cup, or a phone book, or mail-order catalogs, or the mail, or that blotter and pen set that Aunt Mollie gave you for Christmas, or...you know. Everybody's desktop is different, differently the same. Larry's desk-top has an ashtray on it—for shame!—while Jan's has a long-ago emptied can of Diet Dr. Pepper and yours has a couple of rolls of Lifesavers, a bag of chocolate-chip cookies, the grocery list and a collection of coupons.

THINGS TO SPEND MONEY ON

There are all kinds of things you don't need until you get them, and then you can't live without them. They are mostly inexpensive, and you might put them on Christmas or birthday lists.

- Pullout trays fit under the near edge of a standard-height desk to lower the keyboard to the proper level and to push the keyboard out of the way when you're not typing.

- Paper holders hold paper, of all things, next to the monitor when you have to retype stuff to get it into the computer.

- Most monitors come with stands that can be tilted and turned, or you can buy one separately. There are also bendable arms to hold the monitor off the desk completely, but they have to be attached securely to the desk.

continued...

- Other stands allow the computer to sit on its side or to lift the printer off the desktop.

Cigarette smoke is as bad for your computer as it is for you, and so are cookie crumbs and spilled drinks. If you can't stop smoking, at least do it away from the computer. If you can't stop eating and drinking, at least do it where crumbs and drops won't fall into the keyboard. If you ignore this advice, welcome to the club.

Although they are called desktop computers, the desktop is a rotten place to put them, especially the keyboard. For comfort and health's sake, a keyboard should be 26 to 27 inches above the floor, while the surface of a standard desk is about 30 inches above the floor. If you don't type a lot, you can get away with the standard height. If you do type a lot, the standard height will be uncomfortable at best, dangerous at worst.

If there's room, you can put the main box next to the monitor, rather than under it, to make the sight line better. A box that takes up too much horizontal space can be placed vertically. Some "authorities" warn against this, but we never had the slightest trouble with two successive computers standing on their sides, at least not trouble that was caused by standing them on their sides. Do make sure, however, that the unit is not easily tipped over.

If your main box is one of those tall towers, it can go on the floor next to the desk, or even under it. Remember, though, you have to be able to reach the drive slots to insert and remove floppy disks and CD-ROMs. Also, if you often have to open the box to put new things inside—we hope you don't—you have to be able to get at the back without a major operation. Remember too that the computer has to breathe. There are slots for air; don't block them.

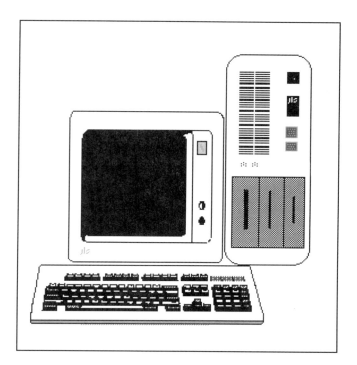

Figure 3.1 Your computer will do headstands if you ask.

The perfect solution may be a desk unit specifically designed to hold a computer—with monitor and keyboard at the proper heights and possibly even room for such peripherals as printers. A local home furniture or office furniture store might have just what you need.

Be careful, though. Some years ago, we bought such a unit from a nearby shop. A high surface provides support for the computer, with monitor atop it, a lower adjustable surface holds the keyboard. A slip-on shelf that can go on either the right or left side provides extra space for clutter and other vital accessories. It was well suited for the kind of computer everybody had when we bought it.

That was before every computer, not just the oddball Macintosh, came with a mouse. There is no surface left on the unit that is big enough to roll the rodent on. We experimented at first by putting the mouse on the adjoining table to the left, which was the correct height but could hardly spare the room. We are both right-handed and had trouble adapting to a southpaw mouse. Finally, we put the mouse on the much too small space remaining on the right of the keyboard and set it to respond to small movements in a big way. (You can adjust the mouse's sensitivity in both Windows and the Macintosh System.) That works fairly well if you are calm, but an impulsive movement will shoot the cursor from the top to the bottom of the screen like a man being shot out of a cannon. Maybe next we'll try putting the mouse on our laps. (The less said about that the better.) A trackball may be the answer.

The period of our custom computer desk was also before computers were as high as many hot-shot machines are now. The monitor sits much too far up. We don't expect you to be able to predict the future course of technology—God knows we can't—but there is no such thing as too much adjustability or too much room to grow, just too much money.

A recent newspaper article made much of a woman who parked her computer on a rollable desk with power sockets in its legs. It cost $900; you can buy a good printer for that.

Still, it is a matter of personal taste, personal needs, and money. For some people, a table salvaged from a garage sale, with a high-end laser printer on it, is ideal. For others, that rollable power desk, with a low-end inkjet printer on it, is a better combination.

In a home office that is clearly separated from the rest of the house, and never visited by clients, make-do may well do. A home office where clients drop in, or one that is part of the house you live in, like the dining room or living room, may call for more decor. There are pieces of furniture to hold your computer, printer, and accessories that, when closed, will pass in anybody's living room. If you have a big closet that can be freed of clothing, brooms, and household junk, you can buy, make, or have made shelves and cabinets to transform it into working space. When guests drop by, close the door.

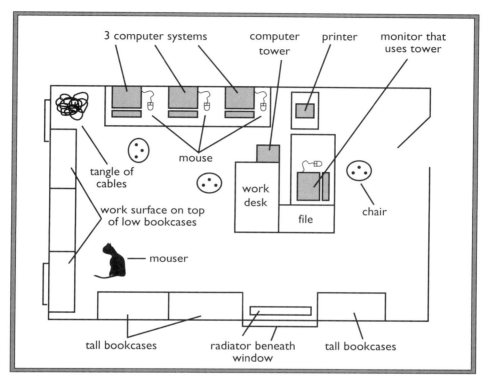

Here is a full-sized home office in an 11-foot x 20-foot room used for little else. What was once a bedroom now holds four computers, two or three more than most home businesses need, with one printer connected to three of them. Although in this case they aren't, the computers could be networked to expand hard disk space and share programs. The desk arrangement provides separate work areas for two people, although three might be able to use the office. It would be crowded but not uncomfortable. Even with four desks and nine running feet of work space on top of the low bookshelves, there is not enough desktop room (there never is).

THE PRINTER STAND

There must be a place for a printer too, maybe on the same table as the computer, maybe elsewhere. There are limits on how far away from the computer the printer can reliably operate—10 to 15 or 20 feet, no sweat in a typical home office. There are also limits of comfort and convenience. It is sure nice to be able to press the control buttons on the printer, put in fresh paper and remove printed sheets without having to get out of your chair, or at least without having to commute. That is one reason why a small space is better than a large space in many ways; a small space must be well-organized and neat, or should be, while a large space can get out of hand.

At the same time, a dot-matrix printer is a noisy beast. You may not want that jackhammer pounding away right next to your ear. Noise is not a problem with laser or inkjet printers, but laser printers in particular need room to breathe. They use heat (300 degrees and more) to bond the image to the paper by melting the toner. You don't feel the heat, but the printer does. It is not smart to shorten the life of a machine that cost five hundred to a thousand dollars or more.

THINGS TO SPEND MONEY ON

- A/B Switches. These are boxes into which you plug two computers and one printer, so you can use two computers with one printer just by flipping a switch (from A to B) instead of by unplugging and reconnecting the cables themselves, which is both a nuisance and a good way to wear out the connectors. You can also get A/B switches to connect one computer to two printers, say a dot matrix for rough drafts or multiple copies, and an inkjet or laser printer for the good stuff. There are also electronic A/B switches, which recognize which machine wants to use which other machine without making you flip anything; A/B/C/D switches, which connect two machines to four other machines, and, for all we know, A/B/C/D/E/F switches.

PLACES FOR THE OTHER STUFF

The modem doesn't require much room. Indeed, if it is an internal modem—one that is installed inside the computer—it doesn't take up any room at all.

There are good arguments on both sides of the internal versus external modem debate, as there are good arguments on both sides of most debates. An internal modem doesn't take up desk space, but it lacks the eight or so lights that flash on and off to tell you what it is up to, if you bother to learn what the lights are saying. An external modem occupies precious real estate—the two in our office take up about six inches by nine inches each, almost as much room as a mouse wants to rove in—but have great Star Wars–looking flashing lights and, more importantly, can be moved from one computer to another without opening the main box and fumbling around among things that can harm you if you don't harm them first.

The modem must be attached to the telephone line and, if it is an external unit, to the power line. It is easy enough to attach the modem to the telephone line. Just drop in to Radio Shack or practically any hardware store and buy a line that is long enough. The limit is not length—the modem could plug into a telephone connection in the next room—but appearance and safety. A telephone line stretching from one room to another looks lazy and unprofessional, and is an invitation to an accident. Even energetic and professional people have accidents. So the modem is plugged into a nearby telephone connection, and the telephone is plugged into the modem so you can use both.

Of course, you have a separate phone number for the business. Otherwise, little Jessie may answer the phone for Ryan Metropolitan Consulting Corporation with a childish "hewwo," or you may answer "Ryan Metropolitan Consulting; good morning" when Mom is calling to make sure you are eating your prunes. Anyway, you have a separate business line for the telephone, the answering machine, the modem, which may also double as a fax machine, and for the real fax machine if you have one. If the phone rings, you answer it. And maybe hear the irritating sound of a fax at the other end. Or someone calls, and you don't answer the phone because you're walking the dog or in the bathroom. And the caller gets to hear the irritating sound of a modem at your end.

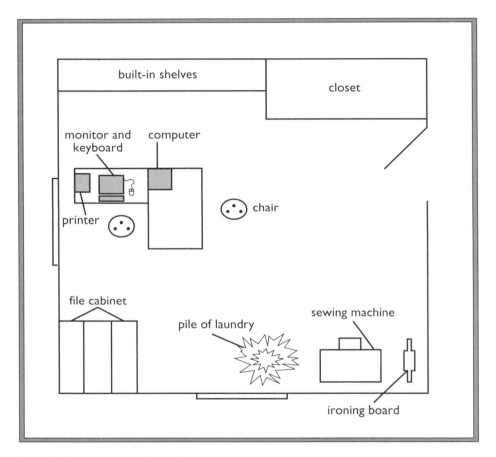

This 12-foot-square office shares space with laundry waiting to be folded and ironed. (Who does that anymore?) It is not a good idea to put the office in the room where you actually wash and dry the laundry; powdered detergent, bleach and lint can creep into computer equipment. But it isn't a bad idea for that little-used room to serve more than one purpose, the main one being your office.

There are devices into which you can plug the telephone line and other gadgets that share the telephone line. They recognize whether the incoming call is a person or a machine and switch to the appropriate device automatically. Of course, there goes more desk space, not to mention money.

ELECTRICITY

All these things need electricity. The computer needs electricity, and it must be plugged into it. The monitor also needs electricity. A monitor may plug into the computer, and not need a separate wall plug, or it may need its own wall plug. An internal modem gets its electricity from the computer; an external modem gets its juice from a wall plug. Its own plug, in fact, may be one of those oversized power converters, or transformers, that blocks two electrical slots. The fax machine needs electricity. The desk lamp needs it. So does the radio on which you listen to Mozart and the television set on which you watch C-SPAN. (So do the radio on which you listen to the Boss and the television on which you watch Oprah.)

One solution for this problem is an extension cord, or several extension cords, and multiple sockets into which you plug everything until you stumble over an extension cord, trip a circuit breaker, blow a fuse, or start a fire that leaves you homeless and business-less, roaming the streets and begging for money and food, checking the garbage cans behind restaurants...forget it.

Another solution is a power strip, a device into which maybe six plugs go but that requires only one wall outlet. Of course, if you turn on everything at once you can still end up in the cast of Les Misérables, but who aside from a teenager listens to the radio and watches television and plays a CD and SimCity all at the same time?

There are three kinds of power strips: plain ones without surge protectors, plain ones that say they have surge protectors, and ones that really have surge protectors. Surges are momentary increases in the strength of the incoming electricity that can blow out a $1 light-bulb or a $3,000 computer—either one, they don't care. If electrical surges are a problem in your area, get one of the costlier power strips; it isn't perfect protection, but it helps.

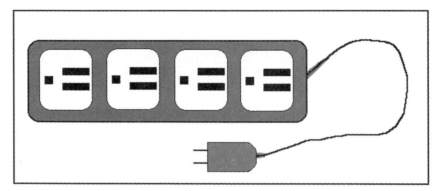

Figure 3.2 Powerstrips turn old houses into computer-friendly spaces.

Or consider hiring an electrician to put in a separate line with surge protection for the home office, if not the whole house. Of course, we are talking real money here.

The computer equipment should also be grounded; most newer homes have those three-slot plugs and most computers have the three-prong plugs that, together, ground the equipment. If your home or apartment is older, it may have two-slot wall plugs. You can buy little adapters to convert three-prong plugs to stick into two-prong slots, along with a wire to attach to a screw in the faceplate to ground things. You may get away with this semisolution. Then again, you may not.

Finally, if you live where the power goes off or plunges in a big way every once in a while, you can get a UPS. This is not a delivery company, but an *Uninterruptible Power Supply.* A UPS is a rather expensive device with a rechargeable battery in it that goes between the power supply and the computer. If the electricity from the utility company fails because Dino fell asleep on the job, the UPS takes over, giving you time to save that document you've been working on and shut down the computer in an orderly fashion. You don't have to move to the middle of nowhere to enjoy power drops. A computer on the same line as a big appliance—an air conditioner, for one—that cycles on unpredictably can suffer sudden amnesia.

This section is starting to sound like it was written by Benjamin Franklin, but we have to add something about lightning. Lightning doesn't have to hit the house to damage the computer and other electrical devices. A nearby bolt can zap a chip. In a thunderstorm, don't merely turn off the computer, the laser printer, and the other modern wonders. Unplug them. (It is a lot easier to unplug one power strip than half a dozen devices plugged in all over the place.)

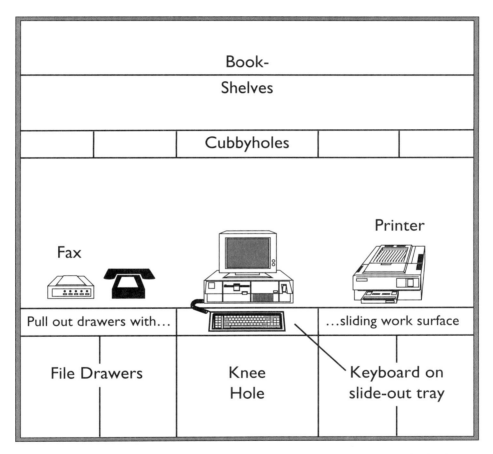

Here is an office in a closet 6 feet wide and 24 inches deep. It can be built into an existing closet, or an office-closet can be added in the corner of the living room or dining room. It's tight, but usable, and ideal for apartment dwellers. At the end of the day, you can close the door and feel like you left the office behind. When friends come to call, they may not even know you are hiding an office behind that louvered door or carved Chinese screen. The small space calls for neatness and organization, and that's a plus.

At the other extreme from lightning is static electricity, which can scramble a floppy disk or poach a chip. Don't stroke the cat and then pick up a floppy. If you must open the computer to poke around inside, ground yourself first. Touching the metal frame of the computer, or an adjacent radiator, will usually suffice.

RUNNING HOT AND COLD

Finally, too much heat or humidity, or too much cold is bad news for all this stuff. The rule of thumb is that if you are too hot or too cold, then so is the computer system, and you should shut everything off and take a walk. But you may be more tolerant of heat or cold than a hard drive or laser printer, so the recommended temperature range is around 50 to 100 degrees, and the recommended maximum humidity is 90 percent. And that is why the attic or basement is rarely the best place for a home office built around a computer. Most of them are too hot or too cold too often.

DISK ORGANIZATION

ORGANIZING FLOPPY DISKS

If your business has gone beyond the shoebox and big-pile-of-papers filing stage, you have filing cabinets and manila folders to keep things in order. Some people are obsessed—rightfully—by organization. The rest of us are more easy-going, which is a polite way to put it. The computer requires still another level of organization.

The things you create at the keyboard and save on the hard disk should also be saved on floppy disks against the day when the hard disk fails, which it will. The floppy disks should be organized. That is, you shouldn't save everything as you create it on one floppy disk until that disk is full, and then save everything subsequently created on a second floppy disk until that one is full. That would be like filing every piece of paper in the A manilla folder until it was full, then saving the next sheets of paper in the B folder until it filled up.

The disks should be organized, and labeled: *Clients 1994, Clients 1995, Proposals 1994, Proposals 1995, Scams 1994*...whatever suits the business. And the disks should be put in something, not just left lying around in piles. Every computer shop and many other stores sell plastic disk containers with semitransparent tops in which stored disks are relatively safe. But the disk holders are designed to make it easy to get at a disk because they go back to the days before hard disk drives were as affordable as VCRs.

In those days, when you wrote a letter you put the word-processing floppy in one drive of the computer, and the floppy on which you wanted to save a copy of the letter in the second drive. When you switched to figuring out the budget, you took out the word-processing floppy and put in the spreadsheet floppy. Usually things were even worse than that, because the word-processing or spreadsheet floppy was often two or three floppies that had to be switched now and then.

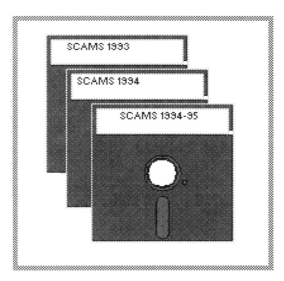

Figure 3.3 Floppies can be as organized or disorganized as your filing cabinet.

Most of the floppy disks we use now store either the original programs that we bought and copied to the hard disk, spare copies of those floppies, backups of files that are on the hard disk, or copies of files that we may never need again and so removed them from the hard disk to make room. In other words, the floppies will only be needed in an emergency, and they can be stored in anything that keeps them safe, not something that makes them easily available day after day.

See if your computer shop sells holders that are cheaper than the ones in the front of the store, or check the racks in a general office-supply outlet.

Every box of floppies comes with warnings telling what you shouldn't do with them:

- Never keep them near magnets (telephones, speakers, lots of stuff you wouldn't think of)
- Never leave them out in the hot sun (the glove compartment or trunk) or cold snow (an unheated basement)
- Never open the slide on 3.5-inch disks or touch the exposed part on 5.25-inch disks.

  The 3.5-inch floppy disks in their rigid containers are much sturdier than the 5.25-inch disks in their paper containers. But the round recording tape inside is equally vulnerable in both.

HARD DISK ORGANIZATION

Now that your physical office is perfectly comfortable and exceedingly well organized—ours isn't either—it is time to organize your computer. Left to itself, a computer is as much of a slob as your favorite uncle, and you have to help it be neat.

In a car, we can travel much faster than we can on foot, but not unless we keep it fueled and in repair. With an axe, we can bring down trees much more efficiently than we can with our bare hands and arms, but not unless we keep it sharp. Most of the tools humans have been devising for thousands of years are extensions of our physical strengths and senses: We can see farther with a telescope or nearer with a microscope than we can with our unaided eyes.

THINGS TO SPEND MONEY ON

- Static control chair or floor pads are a good idea, especially if you have a wool rug. Static electricity is bad for disks and chips.

- Lumbar pillows to support your back come in various sizes, shapes and colors. Footrests help you maintain good posture.

- Mouse pads may provide better traction than the surface of the desk. You can buy them or, when you go into a shop to buy paper, toner, or other supplies, ask for a free one. Or you may get one as a gift. Mouse pads have become so mainstream that museum shops are selling them decorated with antique maps or the Mona Lisa. Mouse cord holders lift the tail off the table.

- Cans of compressed air, minivacuums (don't use inside the computer), and dust cloths treated to both clean and control static keep things neat.

- Tool kits with demagnetized screwdrivers, tweezers and chip pullers work better than the hammer and saw in the garage.

Well, the computer extends our brains. That doesn't mean computers are smart—cockroaches are positively brilliant by comparison— but they are fast as hell at doing things we find plodding. A moment after we remember the name of a customer and type it, the computer tells us her address and phone number, her last order, and her husband's first name. We had to type in all that information two months ago, but we didn't have to remember it. The computer remembers it for us and, if we typed it in right in the first place, remembers it right.

That hard disk in the computer, which you have assiduously copied onto floppy disks or tapes, must be organized. It doesn't care whether it's organized, any more than your car cares whether it has gas in it. You organize it for yourself.

Let us back up for a moment, into your actual office. Some people pile everything everywhere, stick Post-Its on desks, dogs, and children, scrawl important notes on cocktail napkins, and still somehow get the job done. And some people who act the same way don't get the job done, or get it done only with endless agony. Other people make sure the paperclips in their top desk drawer all face the same way, have different-colored felt-tips for specific purposes, keep meticulous notes, and get the job done, and done perfectly. Other, equally organized people screw everything up. The same habits carry over into computer organization, but computers punish sloppiness much more than cocktail napkins punish sloppiness (unless each napkin represents an actual cocktail).

Within the requirements and limitations of the software we use, we organize the computer. Most personal computers today are organized through the facilities provided by Microsoft Windows or the Macintosh System. Frankly, though, they are both getting a little long in the tooth. They are both based on a metaphor—surely you remember the difference between a metaphor and a simile—in which the screen represents a physical desktop with folders and tools on it. But modern computers are far more roomy than any real desktop, and a new metaphor is badly needed.

MACINTOSH

Pardon us for a digression into history, which is necessary to put things into perspective. Pardon us too for starting with the Macintosh, but that was where the metaphor met the market.

The Mac was the first successful personal computer to offer icons, windows, and a variety of standardized menus all operated with a mouse. A few "folders" on the metaphorical desktop held applications and documents. Within each folder could be other folders, and within the other folders could be other folders, not indefinitely but practically so.

So you could have, to make up a likely example, a folder named *applications*. Within that folder could be separate folders, one for your word processor, one for your database manager, one for your spreadsheet. Open the word processor folder and within that, aside from MacWrite or whatever you wrote with, could be separate folders for *business letters*, *family letters*, *crank letters*, *projects*, *proposals*, and so on. It was a wonderful way to organize things, all made possible by the Macintosh system.

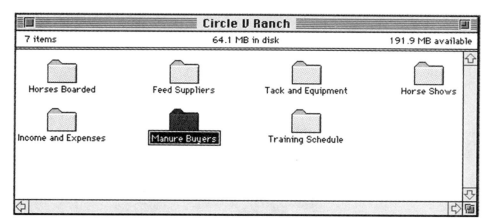

Figure 3.4 One Mac folder holds everything you need, and some things you don't.

The only thing was, you couldn't really do it. Why? Because the original Macintosh had only 128 kilobytes of memory, and stored both applications and documents on 400-kilobyte floppy disks. One floppy disk at a time.

The hotshot Macintosh in our home office, far from the most powerful available, has eight megabytes of memory and a 230-

megabyte hard disk. On that disk, the Mac System can blossom at last. The most recent angry letter to our Congressman, *smithletter2-2-95*, can reside in the *public officials* folder, within the *crank letters* folder, within the MacWrite folder, within the *applications* folder.

It is a perfect tree, with the roots at the top and the branches stretching to the bottom. You are not likely to lose anything in such an organized system. You are probably not going to find it either. At least in a tolerable length of time.

Figure 3.5 Some apple trees grow upside down.

So the Macintosh offers other ways to get started working, including putting the names of programs and documents under the Apple symbol at the top left of every screen, so you can go directly to your destination without passing through every little burg on the way;

making *aliases*, extra icons in handy places that point to the real program or document neatly foldered a half-dozen steps away. Mac users can also view the contents of the hard disk as written lists rather than as icons.

All of these options offer perhaps more convenient methods of finding things. And they also turn a computer that was presented to the world as one that would be as easy to use as a toaster into one that is as easy to use as...well...a computer.

MICROSOFT WINDOWS

It is somewhat harder to get so impossibly well-organized with Microsoft Windows, but it can be done. The next version, Chicago or Windows 4.0 or Windows 95 or whatever, promises to make it easier.

Larry's writing computer is a little portable running Windows for Workgroups 3.11, a version better enough than plain Windows 3.1 that it is worth using even if you are not a member of a workgroup.

The opening screen is the Program Manager, the screen Windows usually opens with, and cascaded in front of it, the Main group, seven icons for little programs for tweaking Windows. Along the bottom of the screen are five little (minimized) icons: accessories, network, games, startup, and applications. By double-clicking on one of those icons, the icons inside them and the programs they represent become available.

Accessories, for example, contains 10 programs that come with Windows, some of which, like *Notepad* and *Clock*, we use a lot, and others of which, like *Object Packager*, we have never even looked at. The point is, the screen looks neat and it is easy to find things and get to work.

In Windows, you can also cascade all these program groups, as the collections are called. Then they look like a stack of index cards you have spread slightly so you can see the titles at the top of each. It makes a pretty impressive display. But who are you trying to impress?

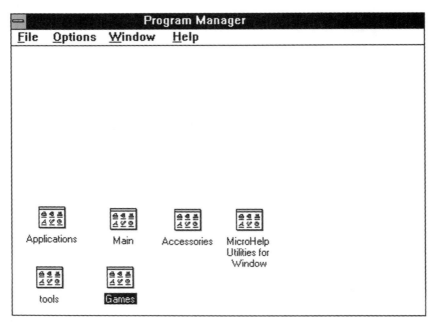

Figure 3.6 The Windows Program Manager.

Instead of cascading them you can tile them, so that each program group gets a little window on the screen next to the others, like the tiles on the bathroom wall. But if you have a lot of program groups, and they are very full, you can't see everything in the windows without a certain amount of mousing around.

PROJECT VERSUS PROGRAM

The Macintosh lets you put all the documents related to one project in one folder regardless of what kind of program each document was created with. In, say, *Mobydick* there are the letters and reports you wrote to ship captains, the spreadsheet of mizzen-mast (whatever that is) expenses you kept, and the database of harpoon suppliers you compiled. If you select the letter you wrote to Captain Ahab, the word-processing program you wrote it with starts and it brings the report to the screen. If you select the mizzen-mast spreadsheet, the program you created it with starts and it brings the spreadsheet to the screen. And so on.

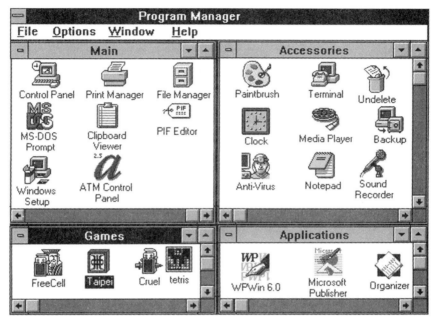

Figure 3.7 Tiled opening screen rivals the mosaics of Pompeii.

There is no way—at least no easy way we have discovered—to do that with Windows. Instead, you start, say, the word-processing program, and then search its list of files for the crucial report. If you decide then to look at the spreadsheet, you start that program and search its list of files. With sufficient memory, however, you can leave the word processor open while you fool around with the spreadsheet or database.

Windows 3.1 offers a written list of the stuff on the hard disk, as the Macintosh does. It is called the *File Manager*, and it is in the Main group. Call it up and you see the list. But it is constrained by the 14-year-old rules of MS-DOS, the original operating system of the IBM-PC and, though much improved, still the operating system of most of the world's personal computers.

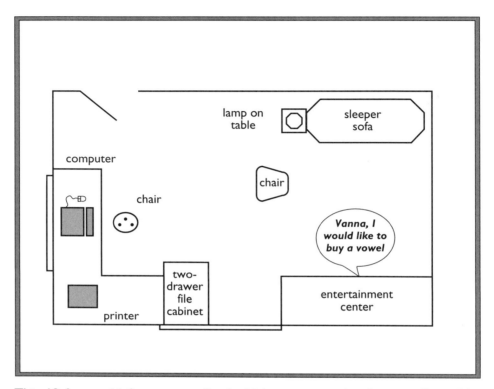

This 12-foot x 16-foot room, all of which was once the den, is still used by other members of the family evenings and weekends and maybe shared with you after school. Your desk and files need not crowd out the entertainment center that preceded them. But, discipline is required not to stop working and watch the soaps.

In DOS, the name of a file can consist of any number of letters up to eight, followed by a period and any number of letters up to three. (The three additional letters following the period, called the *extension*, are optional, although many programs add them automatically.) Believe it, this rule can really test your ingenuity. Should you call the letter proposing marriage to Marge "marmar.ltr?" "marprop.ltr?" "litchka.dee?" Six months from now, will you remember that "marmar.ltr" was the letter you sent after she replied negatively to "marprop.ltr?" Two years from now, will you remember who the Little Chickadee was? Will she remember who "bighunk.ltr" was addressed to?

It is not quite as bad as it sounds. Within each application, programs like word processors and spreadsheets, you can create folders to organize documents. You might have a *letter* and a *proposal* folder within WordPerfect, for example, or an *expense* and a *guess* folder in Microsoft Excel.

Exactly how you organize your hard disk and your office depends on the type of business you are in, your work style, your personality and whatever else is going on in your house. Whatever you decide, do it early before things get too messed up.

SECURITY

Your home office, like your home itself, should be secure. Worries about security are related to both your own psyche and the kind of area in which you live; some people worry too much about security, and some people should. We are not going to discuss smoke detectors, double locks on the doors, or burglar alarms, although those areas are all worthy of attention. So is the question of whether your home-owner's policy covers this expensive business equipment. (Ask your insurance agent.)

Computers add a new level of security problems. Listen, a burglar is not going to rifle your file cabinets or your business records. Unless the burglar is a business rival, and grossly dishonest on top of that, your paper records are valueless. On the other hand, that computer on the desk has value, just as the projection TV or camcorder or silverware have value. You would hate to lose the Rolex Oyster or Cartier bud vase, but you would know what time it is and could smell the flowers without them.

The computer, which you would hate to lose too, contains all your business records on its hard disk: the names and addresses of customers, tax records, proposals, projects. You can replace the bud vase and the computer. You can pick or buy more flowers. You may not be able to replace your business. Can you phone people and say: "I think you owe me money. If you do, please pay?"

There are other ways to lose your business embodied in that machine on the desk. Fire, flood, pestilence come to mind. Burglar and inferno may never strike. The hard disk, however, is certain to fail. Repeat. *The hard disk will fail.*

Eventually, the fuel injector will fail, and so will the dishwasher, the VCR, the power mower, and the hard disk. When the VCR goes bonkers, you get it fixed or—more likely—buy a new one. That collection of Clint Eastwood movies and W. C. Fields classics on videotape don't disappear with the conked-out VCR. You buy a new VCR and play the old tapes again. But when the hard disk fails you can lose whatever is on it. It may be recoverable, with trouble and expense, and it may not be. Please worry about this. We've been making automobiles for 100 years or so, and they still go wrong. We've been electing Congressmen for more than 200 years, and...

There should be up-to-date copies of everything on the hard disk somewhere else, too. The most convenient backup device is a tape drive, and they are discussed in Chapter 4. Copies of everything on the hard drive are made on tape cartridges the first time around, and then copies of the files that have changed since the last copying session the next time around. These backup sessions should be frequent; how frequent depends on your business. If you could bear to lose a day's work, you might back up the hard drive at the end of the day. If you could bear to lose a week's work, back up at the end of the week. If you could bear to lose a month's work, you probably aren't working much anyway. It is all a lot of trouble, but not as much trouble as it sounds. The devices and software can be set to make the copies automatically, after you quit for the day or the week or whenever.

For really critical material, or perhaps because your lawyer or accountant advises it, there should be two backup copies. One copy in the office or another room of the house, where you can get at it in a small emergency, and the second copy away from the office, where you can get at it in a big emergency. By "away from the office" we do not mean in the kitchen. We mean at a friend or colleague's house, in a safe-deposit box, somewhere where it would be safe if your house burned down. Big companies pay to have their computerized records stored in underground bunkers safe from nuclear attack, but that is carrying things a little too far for most home workers.

The preceding was the obligatory drill on backing up a hard disk. Realistically, you are probably not going to back up the disk as religiously as you should or as often as you should. We don't either. So do the following, at least. At the end of the day, put a floppy disk in the computer, make copies of the files you created or modified that day, and put the floppy somewhere else. The cookie jar might do. A sealed fire-proof cookie jar would be better. We all have one of those.

Another aspect of computer security is connected to on-line services, discussed in Chapter 7. CompuServe, America Online, even the Internet if you are brave and have the time, can be great social and economic boons to the home worker. There are answers to technical questions, people with whom you can chat about business ideas, vast information resources. But the exchanges of messages are not private, even though they often feel like it. Assume that anyone can read what you put on line. It is not quite true, but true enough.

If you can't decide what kind of new modem to buy, ask your on-line sources. If you need telephone marketing ideas, ask your electronic penpals. But if you have a great idea for making money, one, perhaps, that no one else has thought of, keep it to yourself. People with computers are like everybody else, and you already know what everybody else is like.

REMINDER LIST

AVOIDING INJURIES

- Don't type too long without a break. Do keep wrists straight and lower back supported.
- Don't sit close to the system box or monitor. Take special care not to sit close to the sides or back.

DESK ORGANIZATION

- Do have comfortable furniture. Regular home and office furniture may do. But equipment designed for computers and peripherals may be better.
- Do buy power strips as an easy and cheap way to provide extra electrical outlets.
- Don't get too hot or cold.

DISK ORGANIZATION

- Do file things on floppy disks.
- Do organize your hard disk. The Macintosh is easier to keep in order, but it isn't perfect. A PC running Microsoft Windows is harder to keep in order, but it can be done.
- Do protect data with regular backups.

SECURITY

- Do keep your equipment safe and your data secure.

THE HARD PART AGAIN

TO DO LIST

✓ More about modems and CD-ROM drives
✓ Sound cards
✓ Speakers
✓ Scanners
✓ Hard drives
✓ Tape drives

If there is no end to computer hardware, there is certainly an end to our time, patience, space, and money. If you have a current (or close to current) PC or Macintosh, with a VGA or better monitor, keyboard, and mouse, a laser printer, a fax modem, and a CD-ROM drive, you probably have all the hardware you need, at least until it becomes obsolete next Tuesday. Not all you want—or all you can find jobs for—just all you *need*.

Before we talk about the other stuff, however, let's backtrack a bit and discuss modems and CD-ROM drives beyond the introductory material in Chapter 1. Many people don't buy a modem or CD-ROM drive when they put together a computer system, or they get stuck with less-than-optimal gear because it came with the outfit.

MODEMS

The key number is 144. Or 14.4. Or 14,000. Or 14,400. All of them mean the modem is capable of sending and receiving 14,400 bits (1s or 0s) per second, called *bps* and sometimes pronounced "bips." That sounds like mucho, but remember that a letter or digit or punctuation mark requires eight bits, or one byte, and that words, and numbers bigger than a few digits, eat up more. The phrase *I didn't vote for her* requires 21 bytes, which is 168 bits, counting the spaces between the words. On a computer spaces are not blanks; they are characters too.

That key number, 14.4 or whatever they call it, is a *minimum*. Don't settle for 9,600 bps (although that is acceptable for sending faxes through the modem), and certainly not 2,400 or 1,200. (Some ads and salespeople call bits per second the "baud" rate. Technically, they are wrong. They just mean "bps.")

You can send data through a speedy modem at a slower pace, and often may do so because the modem at the receiving end can't handle the faster rate or because the on-line service you subscribe to charges more for higher speeds. But you can't send data through a slow modem at a swifter pace. Again, a modem operating at 14,400 bps is the suggested minimum; get a faster one (28,800 bps is next) if you can get it at an acceptable price.

Modems seldom wear out, so buying a faster and more expensive one now is cheaper than buying a slow one now and a faster one a couple of years down the road.

There are other important unintelligibilities, V42/V42*bis* and MNP5 among them. But we recommend that you limit your buying to major brands—Hayes, U.S. Robotics, and Zoom are among the top brands of modems—then, unless you are a technological sophisticate or enjoy playing around with things like this, you probably don't have to worry about them. *Probably*.

INTERNAL VS. EXTERNAL

There is also a reason for buying an external, rather than internal, modem: you can switch it to a second or replacement computer far more easily. The only difference between PC and Mac external modems, the ones that come in their own cases, are the cables that attach them to the computer box and the software that runs them.

Internal modems are special; they must fit in a particular space with the right electrical and data connections. If your computer is a portable, you will probably have to buy the modem manufactured or supplied by the maker of the computer and pay a premium because the maker knows you have no choice. If the portable has a PCMCIA (never mind) slot you may be able to buy a credit-card-size modem to fit into it, but make sure it really does fit and really does work. Not all do. That's another thing you can count on.

PURSE POWER

When you go to an auto dealer, you expect to bargain. When you go to an appliance dealer, you usually don't. Approach the buying of computers and computer add-ons like buying a Mustang, not a Maytag.

continued...

Homework helps. There's nothing like having an ad in your pocket for a system from one computer dealer with a lower price when you go to another computer dealer with a higher price. The systems should be the same, though. Better yet, the cheaper system should be better.

Even without an ad you have power. When you are absolutely sure the gizmo is exactly what you need, don't pull out a credit card. Hesitate, say you want to look elsewhere, edge toward the door. Touching a door handle is magic in saving money.

There are magic words too. "Abracadabra" works for magicians. The following lines are often potent for computer shoppers:

- "Thanks for your trouble. But I'll see if I can get a better price at Wade's."

- "That's my limit. Can you throw in the Diarrheaware program?"

- "How about another four megs?"

Be fair. If a salesperson has spent 20 minutes with you, don't go elsewhere to save five bucks on a $200 modem.

Oh, all right. *Don't* be fair.

CD-ROM DRIVES

Like a modem, a CD-ROM drive can be either internal or external. And, as usual, adding such things to a Macintosh is easier than adding them to a PC. You don't have to remember any numbers here, although there are plenty. Double-speed (300K) is the minimum; triple or quadruple speed are better, but not necessarily better enough to be worth the extra money. If the drive is not at least double-speed, don't even accept it as a gift.

A serious problem with CD-ROM drives, also called *readers*, is that most are designed to hold only one disk. There are drives that hold up to six disks (Pioneer makes one), but they are too expensive for most of us. That one-disk maximum guarantees that when you have the dictionary disk in the drive, you will need the phone numbers disk, and when you have the phone numbers disk in the drive, you will need the road map disk.

Some drives require that the disk be placed in a special cassette, which is then placed in the drive, although that seems to be going out of style. The cassettes are supposed to be easier on both the drive and the disk, and if you have only a few CD-ROMs that you use regularly you can buy a cassette for each of them. If you use a lot of CD-ROMs, that can run into money, so our advice is to buy a drive into which you can stick bare disks. Nothing lasts forever anyway.

Figure 4.1 Apple's PowerCD-ROM drive, with PhotoCD and Audio-CD capabilities, makes the most of multimedia applications.

Most CD-ROM drives these days are advertised as "multisession Kodak Photo CD compatible." That means you can shoot a roll of film and have the snapshots put on a disk as well as on paper and look at them on the computer screen instead of pulling out your wallet or opening a family photo album. If that sounds silly, it's because it is silly. Not silly, though, is incorporating your own photographs or professionally made photographs into computer programs that can handle them. But that is for people and equipment beyond our scope here.

NEC and Toshiba are among the many good names in CD-ROM drives. If you have a Macintosh, you can't do much better than Apple drives.

SOUND CARDS

Unless a PC is sold as a "multimedia" system, the sound is pathetic. It is good enough to beep at you when you make a mistake, and that's about it. The sound built into most Macs is not bad at all, although it can be improved greatly by the addition of a pair of good speakers. But why should you care about sound coming out of your strictly-for-business computer? That's a good question, even if we asked it ourselves.

One answer is, maybe you shouldn't. Still, most games provide sound, and not just chattering guns and whooshing spaceships anymore, but music and dialogue. A dictionary on a CD-ROM may pronounce the words for you. A CD-ROM drive, a good sound card and speakers, along with simple software, can also play music CDs. If this book sounds like it was written by John Lennon or Paul Simon or Pete Seeger or Barbra Streisand or Rosemary Clooney, that is because we were listening to them through our Mac while we wrote. Of course, you can play the CDs on a regular player with better speakers rather than a computer. That might make more sense. So, again, why sound?

Well, why a computer? You can do the same things with a computer and its peripherals as you did with a typewriter, adding machine, address book, and scissors and paste. Maybe you can do them faster, and maybe you can do them better, but they are the same things. The computer adds another dimension to those same old things, however. Reports look like they were turned out in a print shop; mailing lists are aimed at the people most likely to respond; far vaster amounts of customer information is at your disposal than your address book could ever hold.

Now the computer also is moving into new things, and sound is one of them. We communicated with sound for tens of thousands of years before we learned to communicate with text, and voice is still more friendly. Suppose your report includes a brief spoken introduction by you, with, perhaps—to digress away from sound—a little video of you speaking? Outlandish, you say? Sure. Until the other guy does it first. We don't know what new things computers will lead to, any more than Henry Ford knew that the Model T would lead to suburbs, motels, and extramarital sex, or Marconi knew that wireless telegraphy would lead to "Wheel of Fortune" and home shopping networks.

Most likely, the main reason you will want a sound card is to hear the sounds accompanying CD-ROMs. The simplest solution to the sound card problem, which can get disconcertingly complicated, technically, is to buy the CD-ROM drive and the sound card together in a package. In any case, the key numbers for a sound card are 16 and 44.1. Sixteen means 16-bit and 44.1 means 44.1 kHz. Don't let the numbers get lower than those.

Sound cards must be compatible with the Sound Blaster brand of sound cards, which set the de facto standard. So the other simplest solution to the sound card problem is to buy a Sound Blaster 16 card. At any rate, use that card's price and features as your comparison model to other offerings. Media Vision also makes good sound cards, and Turtle Beach sound cards are so good, and expensive, that you probably can't justify one for business purposes.

SPEAKERS

You can't judge the quality of a sound card by hearing it through a PC's crummy little speaker, or even a Macintosh's not-bad-under-the-circumstances speaker. The only rules with speakers are to buy ones intended for use with a computer, and then to spend as much money as you can manage.

Our first PC with a CD-ROM drive and sound card came without speakers, so we went out and bought a pair of speakers for around $30. Voices are recognizable, but music sounds like music on your next-door neighbor's table radio when he forgot to close the window or tune the radio carefully. Our next computer with a CD-ROM drive and sound card got a pair of $200 speakers. It may not be a Bose stereo system, but it sure is acceptable.

SCANNERS

A scanner takes a picture of something that is on paper outside the computer and, with the help of software, turns it into a digital image (1s and 0s, remember) that can go inside the computer. The image on paper might be a photograph, a drawing, or text like a letter, a page from a book or a clipping from a newspaper or magazine. There are two kinds of scanners we should consider.

FLATBED VS. HANDHELD SCANNERS

Flatbed scanners look sort of like copy machines. You lay the page on the glass or plastic and close the lid. That's fine for single sheets, but not so hot when you want to copy a page from a thickish book without tearing it out.

Handheld scanners are rolled by hand over the image. They don't take up much room, which is always an important consideration in a home office, but they only handle an image a few inches across. And you better have a steady hand that moves in a pretty straight line. (There are plastic gizmos that will keep the path straight, although they won't do much for the shakes.) With the right software you can hand-scan, say, a five-inch-wide image in two two-and-half-inch passes and the program will put them together. Maybe even right.

Figure 4.2 The HP ScanJet 3p scanner is a flatbed scanner.

DRAWBACKS

This is all very fine for graphic images—a drawing, for instance—but what about text? It would sure be nice to scan several pages of text into the computer instead of retyping it. But the text, captured by the scanner, is a graphic image. Your word processor can't handle it the way it can handle stuff you type at the keyboard. It is a picture of text, not text itself.

Until quite recently, a scanner could not really be recommended to people who dealt mainly with text, at least not at the home-office level. Those people would require OCR, or *Optical Character Recognition*, the scanner-software combination that could transform the graphic image of text into real text. It would see an open triangle with a cross line in the middle and turn that into an "A." The problem was, OCR was easily confused. It couldn't recognize many typefaces, and even with those it could recognize it was far from perfect. Sellers of OCR would say reassuring things like, "It's 95 percent accurate," which sounds pretty good. We all should be 95 percent accurate. But if there are 50 characters in a line of text that means that, at best, there will be approximately one error every two lines. That's a lot. And not all the errors are going to be obvious, like "tha" for "the." How about "979" for "989?" Would you catch that when you were proofreading the text? You paid $2,000 for the scanner and $1,000 for the software and it gave you "bitch" for "batch."

Like everything else in the computer field, that is changing rapidly. It changed while we were writing this, and undoubtedly will change still more before you read this.

Now there are scanners suitable for nonheavy-duty use that cost only $500 or so. There is software as low as $100 that doesn't make any more mistakes than you do when you're typing, maybe fewer. If your business could benefit from converting text on paper into text in computer, look at Hewlett-Packard, Canon, and Metrotec hardware, and Ominpage and Wordscan software. We can't go into much detail about this, because we haven't tried it yet, but it definitely looks promising. Just remember, this process asks a lot of a computer, and if you have less than a Pentium or a Power Macintosh, the delay might be unbearable.

A SECOND HARD DRIVE

The hard drive that came with your computer was so big that you could never imagine filling it. A few months later, it was jammed to the attic. Even if you are a relentless disk housekeeper, as was suggested in Chapter 3, it will load up. You could replace it with a bigger drive, say twice as big, or you could add a second drive the same size as the first or—better—twice as big.

Most PCs have the internal connections (IDE or EIDE) to hold two hard drives. All Macintoshes have the internal and external connections (SCSI) for a bunch of extra hard drives. Some PCs can take, or be altered to take SCSI drives, and a few Macs handle IDE drives. The differences between them are important to the people for whom such differences are important. Seagate, Maxtor, and Quantum are leading makers of hard drives. As with computers and other peripherals, there are more different names on the outside than there are different machines on the inside. Torn between a Tom drive and a Dick drive? They may both be Harry on the inside.

There are also hard drives with unlimited amounts of room, not because their size is infinite but because the physical disks are changeable. These are called *Bernoulli boxes*, named after the Swiss mathematician Jacob Bernoulli. The removable disks spin somewhat slower than the usual hard disks, and they don't hold as much data as a big hard drive, but you can buy as many of them as you can afford. Another brand of removable-cartridge drives is SyQuest.

TAPE DRIVES

Early personal computers got their programs from, and saved their data on, tape. The drives were often standard tape drives—the kind you play music on—with special connectors, or slightly modified tape machines made for computers only. The trouble with a tape drive is that you have to start at the beginning of the tape and roll ahead until you find what you are looking for. With disks, floppy or hard, you go right to the data you want.

Tapes were a short-lived computer storage medium. As soon as floppy disk drives got cheap enough, people switched to them, just as people switched to hard drives as soon as they got cheap enough, or to color television sets even before they got cheap enough.

But tapes are the best way to make a backup copy of the stuff on a hard drive, because they hold a lot more information than floppy disks and consequently don't force you to sit there and change disks. Their slow speed hardly matters, because you can set them to make the backup after the end of the workday and go away. The main trouble with tape drives, aside from remembering to use them, is that backups is all they can do. A Bernoulli or SyQuest machine can also serve as an extra hard drive. The big name in tape drives is Colorado Memory Systems, part of Hewlett-Packard. Quarter-inch cartridge (QIC) tapes and drives are the most common and accessible for home and home-business computers.

REMINDER LIST

The general rule about hardware is to get the best you can afford, even if you feel you can't afford it. In the long run, the best saves money. You get more work done faster, and you don't have to replace the equipment as soon.

- **Modem:** rated at 14.4, if not faster.
- **CD-ROM drive:** double-speed, and probably not faster.
- **Sound card:** 16 and 44.1 are the key numbers.
- **Speakers:** you won't get computer speakers as good as stereo system speakers, but don't settle for too little.
- **Scanner:** if you retype a lot of text on the computer, a scanner may be worthwhile. Watch this category. If you produce documents with graphics, scanners give you many more choices than clip art, which is just graphics that somebody else has scanned for you.
- **Hard drive:** there is no such thing as too many, or too big, hard drives. Ones with removable disks can serve as supplementary hard drives or for backups.
- **Tape drives** are better for backup.

THE SOFT PART AGAIN

TO DO LIST

- ✓ Living with software you already have for peripherals you already have
- ✓ Simple ways to do boring jobs
- ✓ Getting somebody else to write your letters
- ✓ Building your image
- ✓ ¿Que pasa?
- ✓ Facing the interface

The hardware discussed in Chapter 4—modems, CD-ROM drives, sound cards, speakers, scanners, hard drives, and tape drives—almost always includes software that is at least adequate. So you might as well use it. Here are a few notes on software for those peripherals, and, following that, a rundown of software you didn't know you needed.

MODEMS

Modems often come with a stripped-down or on-the-way-out version of a standard program, or, for computers with Microsoft Windows 3.1, a link to the little Terminal program built into Windows. Since you are not going to spend much time online, and since much of that time will be spent on a commercial service like CompuServe or America Online, the simple software may well be good enough for everything else. If you become a fanatic, and it happens, look at Procomm Plus for Windows or, for the Macintosh, White Knight or Hayes Smartcom.

For a commercial service, get the Windows or Macintosh software. CompuServe, America Online, Prodigy, and others offer GUIs that they practically, or actually, give away. If you would prefer to type **go mail** and **1** to read E-mail, rather than click on an icon, feel free to do it, but don't complain to us.

CD-ROMS

In one way, CD-ROMs don't require software aside from the stuff that comes with the drive. To be more accurate, each disk you buy comes with the software that runs it.

To install the software on a Windows PC, you pull down the File menu, select **Run**, type in the name of the CD-ROM drive (D: most likely), and then type either **setup** or **install**. If you don't know which word to type, type one of them anyway; if it turns out to be wrong, type the other one. (You can also click the **browse** button and see the names of the files on the disk. One of them will be SETUP.EXE or INSTALL.EXE. Click on the name and then on the first **OK** and then on the second **OK**. But what kind of fun is that?) On a Macintosh, you double-click on an icon and then follow the directions. Don't install a CD-ROM if there's an unsaved file open; the programs usually restart the system to take effect.

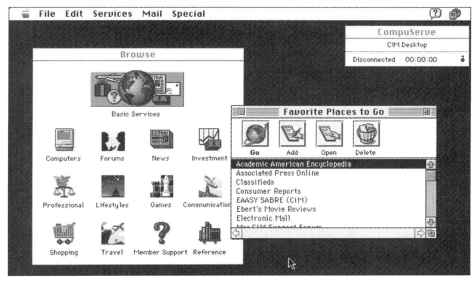

Figure 5.1 Some things in life are free. On-line services sometimes throw in the software.

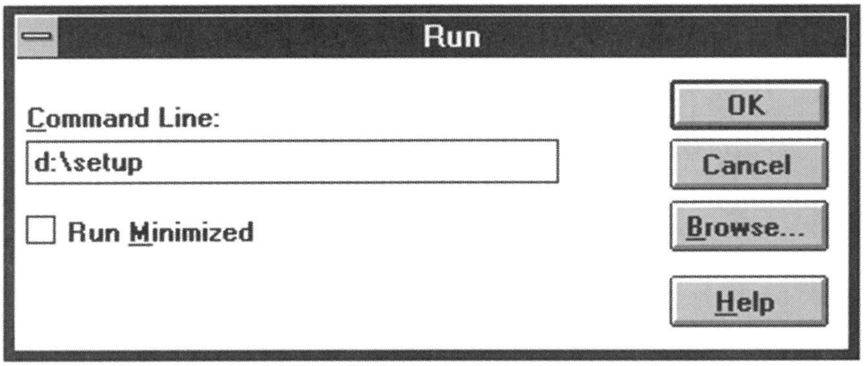

Figure 5.2 Installing software has gotten pretty easy.

Even though CD-ROMs hold far more data than any hard disk, the hard disk is not spared from carrying its part of the load. The Random House Unabridged Dictionary that is in the CD-ROM drive of the Macintosh Quadra this is being written with contains 51.1 megabytes of data. The dictionary is all text; the publisher chose not to fill the remaining 500-plus megabytes with graphics, animations, sounds, and movies. The advantage is that the same disk works in both a PC and a Mac. The fancy stuff doesn't carry over from one type of computer to another. But the software that must be on the hard disk to run the dictionary takes up 783 kilobytes, a pretty fair stretch of space.

Over on the 486, the Allegro Home PC Library, a reference CD-ROM, stores a mere two megabytes, but the software on the hard disk occupies almost 827 kilobytes. So it takes close to a megabyte to run only two megabytes. Two *simple* megabytes. And you thought a 200-megabyte hard disk would never fill up.

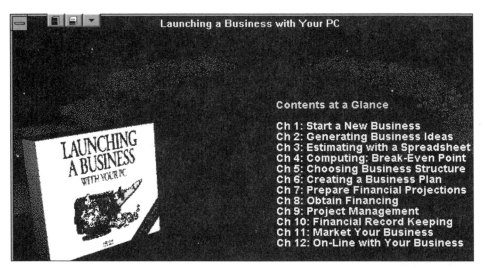

Figure 5.3 A wealth of business information is now available to your computer.

SOUND CARDS

There is no reason to think that the sound card in the 486, a Pro Audio Spectrum 16 from Media Vision, is unusually demanding, but the software that comes with it requires six megabytes of hard disk space. The "User's Guide," a thick paperback, sports a 21-page table of contents. Opening the guide at random brings: "A portion of the sound card is dedicated for Sound Blaster compatibility and is preset to DMA 1 and IRQ 5." Translation: "Buy a computer with the sound card and software already installed."

SPECIALIZED SOFTWARE

Now for the good part. As we said at the beginning of the last chapter about hardware, you already have all the software you really need. With a major word processor, spreadsheet, database manager, maybe one or two desktop publishing and/or presentation programs—or an integrated program, combined perhaps with a major stand-alone—you can do anything that General Motors or the Pentagon can do. But there are easier ways to do routine tasks.

The MySoftware Company puts out a series of programs each of which does one thing, usually one plodding thing. MySoftware says that you can learn any of its programs in about five minutes. If it takes you three times as long, what difference does it make? The programs come in two series, MySomethingoranother and MyAdvancedSomethingoranother, and they sell in the $20 to $70-or-so range. There are programs for making charts, mailing lists, labels, invoices, databases, and for backing up a hard disk. The programs are available for Windows, Macintosh, and plain DOS computers, but not every one for all three. Some also come on CD-ROMs. MyAdvancedLabelDesigner (what a mouthful!), for example, includes 1,000 images and borders to gussy up YourAdvancedLabels.

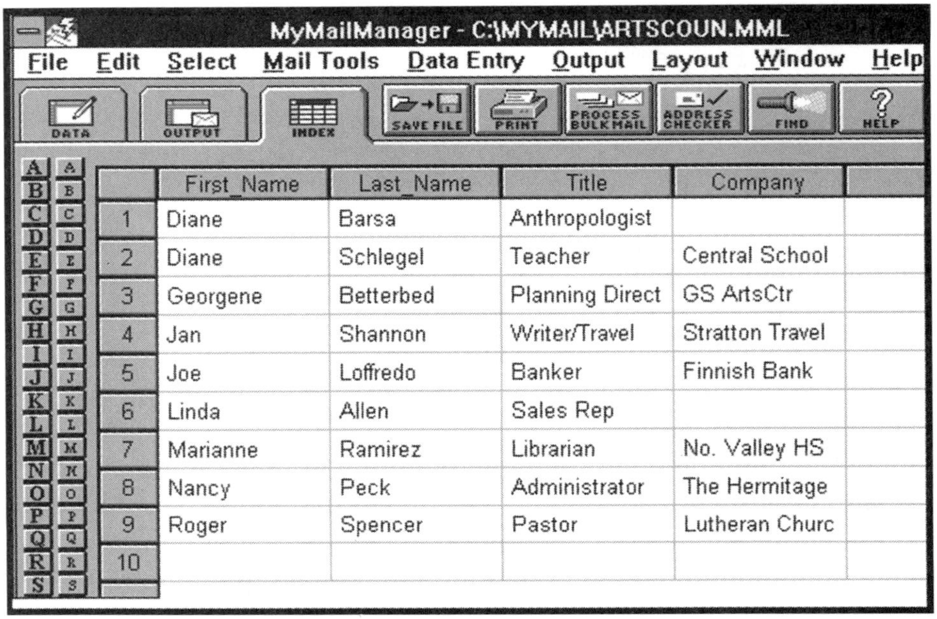

Figure 5.4 Some specialized software might be just right for your business.

PHONE LISTS

Businesses that do a lot of mailings can have what amounts to all the phone books in the country on a few CD-ROMs. If you sell cashmere sweatsocks, the disks can give you Scarsdale, N.Y., or Beverly Hills, Calif., names, addresses, and phone numbers. If you sell beer...well, let's skip that one. DAK Industries and ProCD are among the suppliers.

MODEL LETTERS

If you do a lot of mailings—and even if you don't—it helps to be able to write a good business letter. The fact that you can't write a good business letter doesn't mean that you aren't a good business person and an admirable human being, but it sure leaves that impression. Especially bad is not being able to write a good business letter and not realizing it.

Collections of model letters go back a long time. The back pages of 19th- and early 20th-century popular books often contained ads for collections of love letters, winning words that could be copied with Ms. Right's name in the appropriate places. (The books also had ads for collections of ethnic and racist jokes. Are love letters politically incorrect in the 1990s?) Anyway, there are still collections of letters—for making business not love—and you don't even have to retype them. They come on disks, and can be brought into a word processor and edited to suit your business.

LOVE LETTERS

With directions how to write and when to use them. By Ingoldsby North.

"This is a branch of correspondence which fully demands a volume alone to provide for the various phases incident to Love, Courtship, and Marriage. Few persons, however otherwise fluent with the pen, are able to express in words the promptings of the first dawn of love, and even, the ice once broken, how to follow up a correspondence with the dearest one in the whole world and how to smooth the way with those who need to be consulted in the matter.

Paper Covers 25 cents

Cloth 50 cents"

—excerpt from an ad in the back of a book published in 1902

One such collection is Professional Letterworks, from Round Lake Publishing of Ridgefield, Conn. There are about 250 documents for physicians, lawyers, dentists, and certified public accountants. The book accompanying the disk amounts to a short course in self-promotion.

Sales LetterWorks, also from Round Lake, contains more than 300 letters, memos, and proposals both in print and on disk. The 15 chapters have titles like *Proposals and Quotations*, *Selling by Direct Mail*, and *Communicating with Sales Force*. Each chapter opens with a short introduction, and each letter is accompanied by tips on producing effective documents. You find a letter close to the one you want to write, load it into your word-processing program, and edit it to suit your own requirements. None of the letters are longer than a page, which is a fine idea for business letters.

PUBLICITY KIT

Speaking of self-promotion, there's Publicity Builder from Jian, a course in how to win editors and influence reporters. This sounds like a job only big-city big media people should consider tackling, but it's not. It's much easier to get publicity in a suburban or rural weekly, but only if you do it right, and the publicity can bring business. The book-disk combo deals with "developing your P.R. message" (goals, language, product and company positioning); writing press releases, press kits and case histories; targeting; pitching a message by phone, letter, electronic mail and fax; offering review products and staging demonstrations; following up, and, in great detail, preparing for and attending conventions and trade shows. Jian also offers templates that you use in your usual word-processing or spreadsheet program: Bizplan Builder is for writing proposals; Partners LTD and P.P. Memo are limited-partnership and capital-raising documents, respectively; Cash Collector contains documents for dealing with deadbeats.

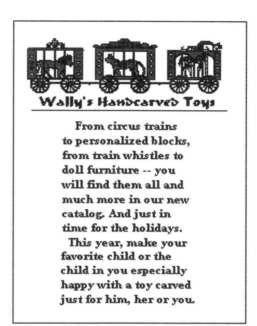

Figure 5.5 Boilerplate letters can be tailored to fit your products or services.

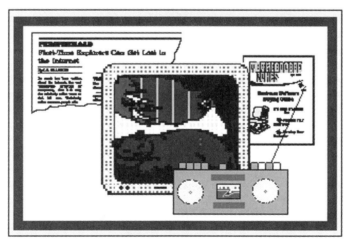

Figure 5.6 Public relations helps build your business.

FOREIGN LANGUAGES

If you must often write in a foreign language, the three major word processors (Microsoft Word for Windows, WordPerfect, and Lotus Ami Pro) offer add-on modules or complete versions to handle different alphabets or specialized accent marks. Contact the publishers for details. If a major part of your business involves one or more foreign languages take a look at Accent, the so-called Word Processor for the World. It is a Windows program, with the familiar menus across the top of the screen, but the menus can be in any of seven foreign languages: French, Finnish, German, Italian, Russian, Spanish, and Portuguese. It also contains a spell checker in 17 languages, a thesaurus in 9 languages and, if you add the Berlitz Interpreter for Windows, which comes with Accent, a translator in 5 languages. Altogether about 30 languages are supported by one or another part of Accent.

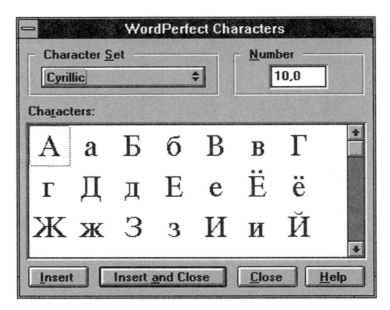

Figure 5.7 Foreign alphabets are available on many word processors.

If your foreign-language needs are occasional and minor, by the way, look at the word processor you are already processing words with. It may well have the characters you need hidden away somewhere. Look through the menus or even—gulp—read the manual. There are also many programs to help brush up your knowledge of a foreign language, or even to learn one from scratch. Hyperglot puts out especially nice ones.

UTILITY PROGRAMS

Then there are programs that improve on the Windows or Macintosh interface. They really do improve on them, although usually in the next version of the official interface Microsoft and Apple try to catch up. These accessory programs may be getting too far into technomania for most home-businesspeople, but they should be mentioned.

Norton Desktop replaces the Windows Program Manager and makes it a lot easier to start programs and manage files. Also included are an antivirus utility, backup, undelete, a defragmenter, a diagnostic program to see what's ailing your hard disk, and a calendar.

Two of these terms require explanation. Except for very short ones, files are stored on hard disks in smallish segments that are not necessarily next to each other. As time goes on and you delete old files and add new ones, the files get scattered around the disk in bits and pieces, with bits and pieces of one file separating B&Ps of another file. The disk is then fragmented, and the heads that search for the B&Ps (not a computer term; just made it up) have to spend much more time doing the job. A defragmenter neatens things up.

Viruses are nasty little programs that screw up a hard disk. They are challenges for a few programmers who have nothing better to do, just as bank vaults are challenges for clever thieves and credit-card receipts left in the trash are challenges for not-too-smart thieves. Antivirus programs fight viruses, obviously, but since there are always new viruses evolving out of the primeval ooze, antivirus programs are always out of date.

Figure 5.8 Viruses make your computer sick, just as they make you sick.

Norton Utilities (also for Macintosh) and The Norton AntiVirus are smaller, more specialized packages.

FROM SNIFFLES TO THE FLU

A computer virus, like a biological virus, can range in seriousness from merely irritating, like the sniffles, to really sickening, like influenza. The computer equivalent of the sniffles might put a message on the screen. The influenza-type might erase files or reformat the hard disk.

A hard disk usually catches a virus from an infected floppy. Once the virus is lodged in the computer's operating system, it infects other floppy disks and, if you then insert an infected floppy into another computer, another operating system. That's how viruses spread, just as colds are spread in schools and offices. You can also catch a virus from software downloaded via modem.

Although floppy disks from big publishers have been infected with viruses, this is extremely rare. You are far more likely to catch a virus from a pirated copy of the program than from the original disks, another good reason for not stealing software.

A worm is a virus that propagates on a network. (Not to be confused with WORM, write once, read many, an optical disk drive for storing huge amounts of data.) A Trojan Horse is similar to a virus but it doesn't reproduce; it looks like a program that does something useful and, in fact, does do something useful—until it destroys your system.

If Norton Desktop is a toolbox, PC Tools for Windows is a whole shop. Aside from an alternative Windows desktop, there are modules for backing up, wiping out viruses, editing icons, getting almost endless information about the system, and more, much more. Yes, you can edit icons, and there are programs to help you do it, but why would you bother?

At Ease, which comes with Macintosh Performas and can be bought for other models, replaces the regular Finder with a simpler arrangement. It is not nearly as useful as the standard desktop, but it has one wonderful advantage: you can set it up so that some programs and documents don't show up at all (unless you know the password), and some things can neither be changed or dumped. If someone comes into the office a few hours a week to type or file, or if the kids write school reports at night on the business Macintosh, you can protect your vital reports and spreadsheets from prying, mischievous, or careless hands. You can even arrange things so the other person can only save data on floppy disks, preserving your hard disk from getting cluttered.

Figure 5.9 You can protect your Mac from the kids—and from yourself.

Another Windows and Macintosh program intended to protect your programs and data, especially from 3- to 10-year-olds, is Kid Desk. It isolates the child from the Program Manager or Finder, replacing it with one of six desktop images, with tools that look like their real-world counterparts: a clock, either digital or analog; calculator, phone and tape recorder, and calendar. Icons appear for programs you have selected for the child. And that's all he or she can play with. The child can't increase his allowance in your family budget spreadsheet, subtract vegetables from next week's shopping list, or insert words learned in the street into the report you have prepared for a valued client. Only a password allows access to the Finder or Program Manager, the real desktop, and you wouldn't be so foolish to make your password "Daddy" or "Mommy" or your first name. At the same time, don't make the password so unguessable that you might forget it.

If the kids are over 10 or so, don't count on anything.

PERIPHERALS

Floppies to Go

Mac-In-DOS for Windows has been in use around here since late 1992, and it is an invaluable program in any workplace, or even a somewhat snug home office, where both kinds of computers are in use. Of course, there are other ways to transfer files from one computer to another, via a network for one. But sometimes the easiest way, the so-called sneaker net, is the least fuss.

With sneaker net, you copy a file onto a floppy disk in a Windows computer, then walk over and slip the floppy into the other Windows computer. Or you copy a file onto a floppy disk in a Macintosh and slip the floppy into the other Macintosh. Mac-In-DOS works the same way, except that you copy a file onto a floppy disk in a Macintosh and slip the floppy into a Windows computer. The screen shows the contents of the Mac floppy on one side, those of the Windows hard disk on the other. A few clicks, and the Mac file is transferred to the Windows disk. (The Macintosh floppy must be a 1.44-

continued...

megabyte disk; the PC cannot make sense out of the old 400- and 800-kilobyte Mac formats.)

The program also works in the other direction, for transferring PC files to a Macintosh. It will also format diskettes for the Macintosh. That does not make much sense if the computers are in the same office, but could be handy if one machine is at home and the other is at work.

The new Mac-In-DOS for Windows, version 2.1, is somewhat easier and noticeably faster. It is a product of Pacific Micro of Mountain View, Calif., phone (415) 948-6200, and is widely available for around $129.

From the Peripherals column, Sept. 13, 1994. Copyright © 1994 by The New York Times Company. Reprinted by permission.

REMINDER LIST

- Don't buy software you don't need, especially if you already have it.
- Still, there is specialized software that never gets bored.
- Somebody has probably already written that letter you're struggling with.
- Publicity doesn't cost anything. Advertising does.
- There are programs that speak another language.
- If your interface is ugly, put a mask on it.

BUYING SMART

TO DO LIST

BUYING HARDWARE

- ✓ Reading the ads
- ✓ Asking questions
- ✓ Credit cards
- ✓ Warranties
- ✓ Where to buy

BUYING SOFTWARE

- ✓ Stick with the leaders
- ✓ It's the price, stupid
- ✓ Piracy
- ✓ Shareware

HARDWARE

It is past time to find the right computer, either for the first go-round or to replace the old one with a fresh model. Before you start shopping you study the ads in the local paper. Here's one that looks good:

Commitment-minded SWM, 48, 6′3″, trim, athletic build…

Whoops! Wrong part of the paper.

Figure 6.1 Read between the lines in ads.

486SX33 FULL-FUNCTION MULTIMEDIA COMPUTER WITH CD-ROM AND SVGA MONITOR

That's from an actual ad. Only the brand name (a well-known one) has been left out. Let's go through the specs line by line, asking the kinds of questions you should ask before you buy a system, whether in person or by phone. You will remember the technical terms from Chapters 1 and 4. If you don't, you can find them in the glossary.

A 486 is the least powerful central processing unit, or CPU, you should buy these days. The SX is a stripped-backed version of the DX, the full 486, which you really should buy, or better yet a 486/DX2/thingamajig, a souped-up cousin of the plain DX.

Thirty-three is the speed of the CPU in megahertz. This chip's heart beats 33 thousand times a second, which sounds faster than blazes but in fact is no longer exceptional.

We don't know what "full function" means, but they hardly would put "half function" or "functionally challenged" in an advertisement.

"Multimedia" means the machine is capable of sound and video, not just text and graphics. There are details later in the ad, but not many, on the CD-ROM drive.

It would also be desirable to know more about the monitor. SVGA is about the best you can get, and a little note at the bottom says "SVGA28," so presumably 28 is its dot pitch rather than its age, which is fine. But what is the monitor's maximum resolution, and does the system box include a card that can wring that maximum resolution out of the monitor? Indeed, what size is it? The ad doesn't even say it is a color monitor, but surely it is. The assumption is that the monitor is a 14-inch one with at least 800 by 600 pixels resolution producing 256 colors, and that the accompanying video card has at least one megabyte of memory (two megabytes are better). But, as the old saying goes, you should never assume. You must ask.

200-MB HARD DRIVE/4 MB RAM EXPANDABLE TO 56 MB

The hard drive can store 200 megabytes of programs and documents, a minimum in a desktop computer today, when an ordinary word-processing program can fill six or eight megabytes of space before you write even a note to the teacher. How fast is the hard drive? Is there room inside the main box for a second hard drive when the first one runs out of space? There are four megabytes of RAM, half the memory you should have, but at least the computer can be expanded to 56 megabytes of memory, far more than you will ever need until you need it.

DOUBLE-SPEED CD-ROM DRIVE/LOCAL BUS VIDEO GRAPHICS

It is desirable to know the precise speed of the drive, but "double speed" probably means it is acceptable. What brand is it? Does it take disks in the nude, or must you dress them in cassettes first? Local bus video graphics means that the stuff that appears on the screen runs through its own circuits, rather than having to share circuits with other data. That's faster.

SOUND BLASTER 16 AUDIO BOARD

Sound Blaster is a top brand in audio boards, and 16, rather than 8, bits is the current standard in sound. It means the computer is capable of matching a fair tabletop radio or CD player, if the speakers are up to it, but hardly a midrange stereo system. Sound Blaster boards don't work with every CD-ROM drive, but presumably these two get along or they wouldn't be packaged together.

BUILT-IN FAX MODEM

It is good that it is a fax modem, but more information is needed. Can the modem both send and receive faxes? Early ones couldn't do both. At what speed does it send faxes? More importantly, at what speed does it send regular data? Is software included to operate the modem, both for regular data and faxes?

PREINSTALLED SOFTWARE MS-DOS 6.2, MS WINDOWS 3.1, TAB WORKS, QUICKEN 2.0, PRODIGY

You can't run a current PC without DOS, and you shouldn't run one without Windows, so you might as well get them with the computer. Preinstalled means that this essential software is already on the hard disk, which saves you the trouble of copying it from the floppy disks to the hard disk. But are the floppy disks for the programs included? It is a pain to make your own copies of those two huge collections, and you absolutely must have spare copies of them right away.

Are the full manuals for DOS and Windows included, or abbreviated versions, or none at all? The official manuals can be tedious, but sometimes you need them.

Tab Works sounds like an integrated program, like ClarisWorks and Microsoft Works, but it isn't. It is a front end for Microsoft Windows, providing a presumably easier-to-use graphical interface than is offered by Windows itself. There are two schools of thought about third-party substitutes for the standard Windows, or for that matter Macintosh, interface. School A says, If you like it, use it. That seems to make sense. School B takes a few more words. If you learn the standard way of working with Windows or the Macintosh System, you can sit down at any computer running one or the other and use them. If all you know is Charlie Works, or Caitlin, or Ed Norton, you are helpless or at least awkward at a computer with the official interface.

Quicken is a best-selling program for personal finances, a very good one for people who like to account for every cent, or at least every dollar. A colleague loves Quicken, but doesn't actually use it because he would feel obligated to account for every red cent. His brother-in-law uses Quicken unobsessively; his biggest category of spending is "misc." In any case, is a personal-finance program suitable for a home business? Maybe, maybe not.

Prodigy is a leading commercial on-line service, and the software will let you get onto it to sign up and maybe receive a limited free run. But Prodigy is a family-oriented service and not at all the best choice for business users.

The illustration with the ad also shows a mouse, two speakers, and a microphone. Nothing else is said about them. There probably wasn't room in the ad. Or maybe the store would rather not say anything about them. Of course, the computer in the illustration includes a floppy disk drive, a 3.5-inch one. But the ad doesn't say. Does it also include a 5.25-inch drive? Probably not, or the ad would say so.

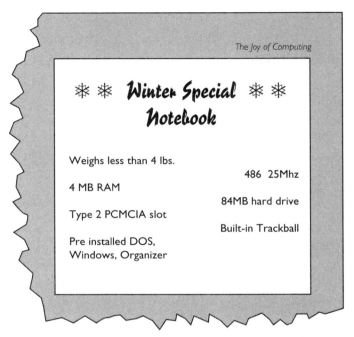

Figure 6.2 Skipping down a few inches to an advertisement for a brand-name notebook.

WEIGHS LESS THAN 4 POUNDS

If it weighs less than four pounds, it probably weighs 3.9999 pounds. That almost certainly means it doesn't include a floppy disk drive at all. You dare not buy a computer without a floppy disk drive. How would you install new software on it? How would you make backup copies of files? So you have to buy an accessory disk drive. How much is it?

486 25 MHZ

That's an underpowered CPU for a desktop computer, but would probably suffice for a portable.

4MB RAM 84 MB HARD DRIVE

Repeat: four megabytes of memory ain't enough. Neither is an 84-megabyte hard drive but, again, it would probably suffice for a portable that is not your only computer, or one that sees limited use.

TYPE 2 PCMCIA SLOT

That is a slot that holds a credit-card-sized board that adds memory, a modem, or a hard drive to a computer without having to open the box up, which you mostly can't do with portables anyway. There are three types, and Type 2 probably means the slot takes a modem. Not all PCMCIA cards work in all PCMCIA slots. What cards are available for this portable, and how much do they cost?

BUILT-IN TRACKBALL

Big deal. Every portable has a built-in trackball, or a substitute that amounts to the same thing. It takes time to get used to one, more than a few minutes' trial in the shop, and you could end up hating it. Is there a serial port or a mouse port to attach a regular mouse?

PREINSTALLED DOS, WINDOWS AND ORGANIZER

Good, you have to have DOS and Windows. The same questions apply as they did to the first ad: Are the original floppy disks and full manuals included?

Organizer is probably Lotus Organizer, a simple and handsome electronic address book with elements of a personal information organizer. It's a pleasant addition to the package, but not an essential first purchase. (But it's not a purchase, it's free.) Lotus Organizer's screens make good use of color, and it is a question how legible it would be on a monochrome screen.

Of course, the ad for the portable doesn't say the screen is mono-chrome, which means that undoubtedly it is. How big is it, by the way?

How long does the manufacturer *say* the computer will run on battery power before a recharge is required? How long does the computer actually run on battery power before a recharge is required? How long does it take the battery to recharge? What kind of batteries and how much do they cost? Did they weigh the computer *before* they put the battery in? Surely an AC adapter is included, but how big is it and how much does it weigh?

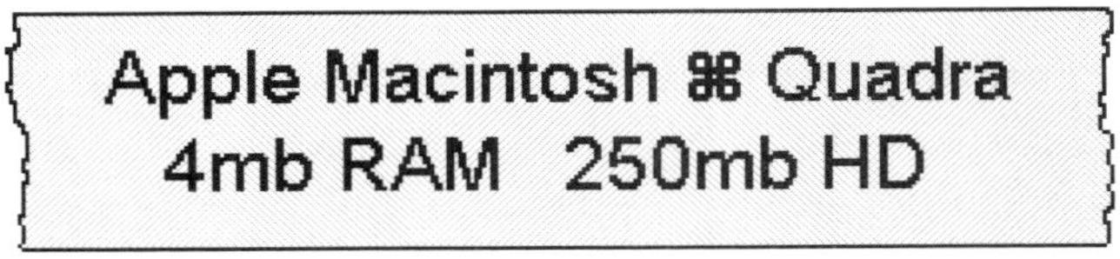

> ## Apple Macintosh ⌘ Quadra
> ## 4mb RAM   250mb HD

Figure 6.3 Here's a Macintosh ad.

APPLE MACINTOSH QUADRA 630 4 MB RAM 250 MB HD

By now, you are weary of hearing that four megabytes of memory is not nearly enough and that a hard disk in the 200-megabyte range is merely acceptable. There is no mention of a monitor. That means it is not included in the price, believe us. Neither is a keyboard. A mouse is probably included, because you can't operate a Mac sans mouse anymore than you can operate an auto without a steering wheel. But neither can you operate a Mac without a monitor and keyboard anymore than you can operate an auto without whatever else you can't operate an auto without.

There is also no mention of software, not even system software. Without system software, the computer is as much use as a tape recorder without tapes, or a lamp without lightbulbs, or a platonic relationship. Finally, though all the Quadras are fine machines, the best Macs you could buy the day before yesterday, it is Apple's stated intention to ease them out in favor of the Power Macintoshes. So there is a pig-in-the-poke flavor here.

YOU CAN'T GO TOO FAR

Our family calculates vacation spending in a rigorously scientific fashion: Jan makes an estimate of how much we'll need, and Larry doubles it. How big a hard disk do you need? That's not a bad method. Let's look at one PC in our office.

DOS. This subdirectory, which is essential, can be pared down if you know what you're doing. Unpared, this one occupies 5,762,572 bytes of space.

WINDOWS. Also essential, and 6,975,689 bytes. There are three subdirectories—System, Claris, MSapps—under it.

- **SYSTEM** These things make Windows programs work. 19,402,449 bytes.

- **CLARIS** This is ClarisWorks, an integrated program. 1,943,870 bytes.

- **MSAPPS** Nothing there, but eight subdirectories under it. Forget them for now.

That admittedly incomplete survey shows that 34,084,580 bytes are used by mostly unavoidable files, and one integrated program that actually lets us get some work done. That's 33,285.7 kilobytes, the calculator says, or 32.5 megabytes.

Add one major standalone program—16 megabytes are not unusual—and we are pushing 50 megabytes before we've written a report, worked out a spreadsheet, or compiled a database.

Add graphics and sounds, notorious space hogs, and a game or three, and the recommended minimum of about 200 megabytes starts to feel cramped. And every year the new programs gobble up more hard disk space.

BUYING STRATEGIES

"Probably," "presumably," "assumption," and "almost certainly" appeared repeatedly in the paragraphs above. Get your questions answered before you draw your credit card. Pretend you are buying a used car.

Speaking of credit cards, an important note in small type at the bottom of the Macintosh ad says "cash or certified check only." It is a very stupid thing to buy a computer with anything other than a credit card. A credit card gives you a chance to have second thoughts, and enlists the bank or other warm and cuddly institution on your side if there is a dispute.

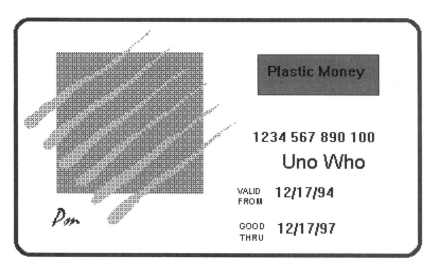

Figure 6.4 Buying with plastic can be insurance against problems.

Some people sign up for any warranty that is offered. Some never do. Whichever makes you happy, we say, you should do. But remember that warranty deals represent an important source of income for retailers because things seldom break down in their first year or two. A particularly critical point about computer warranties is whether the repairman will come to your office, or whether you have to bring the system in to the shop, or even ship it half-way across the country. Transporting a portable is no big deal, perhaps, and packing and shipping it is probably not a major inconvenience, but what about a big desktop? The safest way to pack and ship a computer is in the packing it arrived in, but that means you have to store the original cartons and all the protective dreck that was in them. Do you have the room to store it? Can you really repack everything in boxes that were built around the equipment, without an inch to spare, in the first place?

LET'S BUY A COMPUTER

First, listen carefully. No computer you buy is going to become a family heirloom, passed on to children and grandchildren like silverware and brooches. It will be amazing if it doesn't feel like an antique—a valueless antique—in four or five years, two or three if you're fussy, one or two if you're crazy. Probably there are people using the original IBM PC today, although it went on the market in 1981, or the first Macintosh, born in 1984. But they are Stanley Steamers. A Stanley Steamer could be a lot of fun, but you wouldn't commute in it, and you couldn't call Stanley for repairs. The highly praised 486 we bought less than a year ago came from a mail-order company that has since been absorbed by another, because it was running bright red. An equivalent machine now costs less than half of what we paid. The company that made the excellent CD-ROM drive/sound board in the 486 has filed for Chapter 11.

All sorts of places sell computers. Computer dealers do it, super-stores do it, electronics shops do it, regular department stores as well as discount and office-supply stores do it, the kid down the block does it, and mail-order houses do it. There are advantages and disadvantages to each.

One thing to keep in mind is that no one will recommend a computer he doesn't sell. If you are shopping for a new car and you go to a General Motors dealer, you don't expect the salesperson to say that Ford makes the ideal car for your purposes. If you are shopping for a dishwasher and go to a General Electric dealer, the word "Maytag" will never be heard. We know that truth about cars and dishwashers, because we grew up with them, but it is easy to forget it about computers.

Let's go down the list from best to worst, or maybe the other way around.

Figure 6.5 Like old cars, old computers are a lot of trouble. Unlike old cars, they're no fun.

Computer Dealers

The small- to medium-sized shop that sells one or a few lines of computers, printers, and the other stuff is, like the mom-and-pop grocery store, nearly extinct.

- **Advantages:** The person you deal with probably knows something about computers, at least the brands she sells. You may be able to put together a system according to your specifications.
- **Disadvantage:** You pay more.

Computer Superstores

The big shop with aisles and aisles of hardware may have competitive prices.

- **Advantage:** Price, variety.
- **Disadvantage:** The person you deal with, if you can find a person to deal with, probably doesn't know much about computers.

Electronics Stores

You may feel more comfortable in this place, because you've shopped here before for your CD player and Nintendo.

- **Advantage:** Price, maybe variety.
- **Disadvantages:** The person you deal with almost certainly doesn't know anything about computers. What you see is what you get; it is unlikely that you can put together a customized system. Also, you may go in for a Pentium and come out with a Performa, a microwave oven, a talking wristwatch, and a boom box.

Regular Department, Discount, and Office-Supply Stores

You may feel more comfortable here too, because you're used to them.

- **Advantage:** Price, maybe.
- **Disadvantages:** The same as electronic stores, plus the near-sure-thing that the salesperson doesn't know as much as you do if you've read this far and kept half an eye open. Next spring, he'll sell hoses and lawnmowers, while you will still be running the computer you bought solely because it came in decorator colors.

The Kid Down the Block

He may not be a kid, or down the block, or a he. PCs are made out of standard parts—even IBM and Apple don't make many of the parts of their computers—and a sufficiently knowledgeable or foolhardy person can put one together. It may be a good computer, even a great computer, at a price that shops can't match because of their overhead in rent, heat and air-conditioning, and salaries.

- **Advantage:** That last sentence.
- **Disadvantages:** Just about everything else. If you don't know much about computers, how can you tell if you got what you paid for? What do you do if something goes wrong? Sue his mother?

Mail-Order Houses

That term is old fashioned; hardly any of them send things by mail anymore. UPS-order? FedEx order? If you stick to the big long-established companies, you can probably buy a good computer at a good price. If you opt for the small short-established companies, you also can probably buy a good computer at a better price. You can usually guess how big and well-established a mail-order house is by how big and colorful its ad in a computer magazine is and whether the ad is up front or on the back cover rather than tucked among the truss ads, and if it has been around for a long time in computer terms it will often say "since 1986" in the ad. But if something goes wrong, distance may lead to disenchantment. Although you would never do it, the feeling that you could go to the shop and punch somebody in the nose lends illusory confidence to local buying.

- **Advantage:** Price and, in many cases, customizability.
- **Disadvantage:** Distance.

By the way, the fact that you can't try out the hardware before you buy it is mostly an imagined drawback. There are very few computer retailers where you can try out hardware, at least long enough to tell a real difference. There is also the question of support after you spend your money. You naturally suppose that you can get more and better help from a local retailer than from a telephone number six states away. It ain't necessarily so. Also, read the smallest print in the mail-order ad to look for the phrase "restocking fee." Whether or not those dread words appear, ask the person you talk to on the phone whether there is a restocking fee. A restocking fee is a charge, sometimes a hefty one, for returning hardware no matter why or how much you hate it.

SOFTWARE

You are not going to buy much software, and you are going to stick with the market leaders, so go for price.

The suggested retail price of a software program is a fiction, indeed a damned fiction, and publishers are edging away from listing them. Don't thank them for this trend; it is like thanking someone for not lying for a change. Also, since you ordinarily cannot return software unless there is something gravely wrong with it—otherwise you could buy the program, make copies of the disks, and then get your money back—and since a five-minute trial in the store, if you can even arrange one, doesn't give you any idea of whether you will like the program after a month has passed, again go for price. That means either one of the big software retailers or mail order.

The mail just arrived, with three Macintosh mail-order catalogs. (After you've bought a computer and a few programs, and subscribed to a computer magazine, you will find your mailbox full of catalogs too.) The first catalog offers Microsoft Word 6.0, an excellent program, for $295, or an upgrade for people who have an earlier version of the program for $99. The second, $295 and $95. The third, $298.95 and $119.95. It sounds like the third company is out of the loop. Add $3 for overnight shipping and tomorrow you will have a word processor that can handle anything you are likely to throw at it for around $300.

Wait. The first company is in the state we live in, so it will add sales tax. We will buy the program out of state, and then voluntarily send the sales tax to our state.

Back to reality. A phone call to the nearest branch of a big software chain brought a price of $329.98 for Microsoft Word 6.0. Asked if he had an upgrade price, the salesman said he could get one, but did not offer to do it.

There are two other ways to get software: piracy and, what usually amounts to the same thing, shareware.

Figure 6.6 Don't become a modern-day pirate.

PIRACY

This means you steal the software by making copies of somebody else's disks. The word itself is a giveaway. A pirate is romantic and glamorous. A thief isn't.

- **Advantages:** Piracy costs little or nothing, just the cost of the disks and probably a book on how to use the program, which may well be better than the official manuals that come with the program. Unless you run a big company, or make software piracy a business of its own, you are very unlikely to get caught. So why not do it?

- **Disadvantages:**

  1. You expect customers to pay you for your work, and so do software publishers.

  2. You *could* get caught. That kid who worked part time for you, the one you fired for dishonesty last summer, might turn you in. The publisher, or the Software Publishers Association, an industry group, might decide to make an example of Arf 'n' Barf Kennels.

  3. You don't know who the software was sleeping with before you fell in love with it. Pirated software can contain viruses—malicious little programs written by psychotic nerds—that can infect your whole system and screw up or wipe out everything.

  4. Piracy is wrong. It is not like going through the amber light; it is like doing 75 miles per hour in a 15-mile-per-hour zone.

  5. Finally, for what it is worth, you have no relationship with the publisher, and don't hear about problems, upgrades, or special deals, and you can't call for help. You don't get on mailing lists either. Maybe that's an advantage.

So don't do it. It's for muggers, not Bluebeards.

SHAREWARE

These are programs, some of them as good as conventional commercial programs, and others as bad or worse, which are distributed by word of mouth, or disk of hand, or modem of phone. A guy writes a program and passes it on to the world by putting it on one or more of the on-line services, or distributing it through clubs and publications, and invites people to try it at no cost, and to make copies to give to their friends and colleagues.

- **Advantages:** The program might be perfect for your business. You try it out and, if you continue to use it, you then pay the author. At least, that's what you are supposed to do and a very few people actually do it. Once upon a time it was called the honor system. To make the payment worthwhile, the programmer may send you a copy of the program with more or better features than the one you have, or at least a copy that doesn't remind you that you haven't paid for it every time you run it, or instructions, or the right to phone the author if you have a problem and to be informed of new versions. It is a wonderful idea for selling software, eliminating the costs of packaging, advertising, and distribution. Too bad it seldom works.

    If you find a shareware program that you can use, you should pay for it. The cost is generally modest.

- **Disadvantages:** We don't recommend shareware for home offices because it can be a time-wearing trial finding a suitable shareware program, and there is little or no guaranteed recourse if you encounter a fatal flaw months down the line. If you enjoy that kind of thing, do it. If you don't, don't.

REMINDER LIST

HARDWARE

- Read the ads.
- Ask questions.
- Use a credit card.
- Be skeptical about warranties.
- Buy where you feel comfortable.

SOFTWARE

- Stick with the leaders.
- Price, price, price.
- Pirates walk the plank, too.
- Shun shareware.

STAYING SMART

TO DO LIST

✓ Explore
✓ Read
✓ Ask other people

You want to do your work and make your money, not become saddled with yet another job. But part of your work is done with a computer, and that part changes faster than anything in the world has ever changed before. As the old Chinese curse says: "May you live in interesting times."

Some of the changes can make your work easier or faster or bring in more money. Still, most of them won't make any difference. How do you find out about the ones that will?

EXPLORE WHAT YOU'VE GOT

For a start, look at what you already are using. Most people never get to the bottom of the programs they run all the time. We'll use WordPerfect 3.0 for the Macintosh as an example, because that is what these words are being produced with right now, but the principles apply to any program.

Larry writes a weekly column, often on a Macintosh with WordPerfect, so writing, basic editing, and saving a file are habits by now. Since those are a matter of routine, however, he could use any Macintosh word processor, because they all follow the same basic commands, and any Windows word processor, because they obey similar commands. There is seldom a need to make a printed copy—the column goes from personal computer to corporate computer—but it is just about as easy to make a printout as it is to save a copy of the file on the disk.

LEARN THE BASICS

These are the main things you need to know about any program: how to produce a file, make changes to it, save a copy on a disk, and print it out and/or transmit it through the telephone lines. With that knowledge of a word processor, you can write a business letter or report, make a to-do list or ransom note, save it on the disk, and produce a copy to drop in either the real or electronic mailbox. With the knowledge of the equivalents in any other application—a spread-sheet program or database manager or whatever—you can make them work in a basic fashion. Only the details of entering data will differ; you save and print the same way as with word processors. Those are the first things you should learn, and they can be the last things you learn too. Maybe that's all you need; maybe it isn't.

LOOK INTO THE FEATURES

Modern programs are full of features—too many features, some say—that you might find useful if you knew they were there. How do you discover them? You explore. (Use an extra copy of a file, or a file made for experimenting. Don't risk something you need.)

There are nine named menus across the top of the Macintosh WordPerfect screen: **File**, **Edit**, **Insert**, **Layout**, **Tools**, **Table**, **Font**, **Size**, and **Style**. Under File are **New**, **Open**, **Close**, **Save**, **Save As**, **Print**, and **Quit**. Those are used all the time.

But what are **Open Latest**, **Stationery**, **Insert File**, **Page Setup**, and **Print Preview**? Let's try Print Preview. Wow, a picture of the printed page appears, the type not readable but the shape it forms on the page clear. If this were a business letter, a preview before a printout would give a good idea of the first impression it would have on the recipient when he unfolded it, before he had read a word. It could also save a piece of paper, the printout you throw away because there is room for improvement that wasn't apparent before you saw a printed copy.

Under the Edit menu, among 13 other options, you'll see **Preferences**. Selecting that leads to a window with nine icons for environment, word services, librarian, and others. Librarian? Take a look. Ways to set up the appearance of headers—lines at the top of a page—and footers—lines at the bottom of a page—footnotes, and many more. You probably don't need footnotes, but a line repeated at the top of every page of that report you are sending to the Grundies would look quite professional. Looking quite professional is the whole idea.

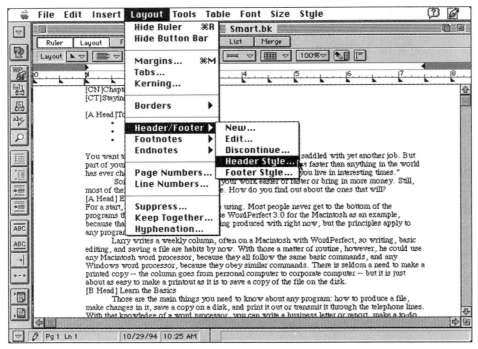

Figure 7.1 WordPerfect for the Macintosh. Look deeper into those menus.

Under the Insert menu, among nine options, **Symbols** shows where to find letters with accent marks. Spelling a foreign word that has accent marks without accent marks is misspelling it.

Altogether, there are 79 things that can be done with these menus, not counting **Style** (didn't bother to try underline), **Size**, or **Font**, where all the typefaces that are available are listed. Maybe the report would look more impressive in Arrus BT Roman (just tried it, and it didn't).

Other programs run deep too. We have created many of the illustrations here with Microsoft Publisher for Windows, and learned a fair amount about it. It is set up for a limited number of standard forms and, after using it for a while, you may ignore other possibilities. The seven business forms in the program may be near-perfect for your needs. But you can also, without much trouble, modify any of the forms into templates that suit you exactly, and then use them over and over again. There is no provision at all in Publisher for a mail-order catalog. But if you want to sell personalized litter boxes by mail, Luisa Simone gives full instructions in *Microsoft Publisher by Design* (Microsoft Press) for designing a catalog with tools already in the program. (Her example is Epicurean Delights, edible flowers.)

You want to keep a computerized file of index cards? Before you go out and buy another program, look at Cardfile, which comes with Windows. It's not very powerful, but maybe you don't need much power. You already have Cardfile.

We are both good spellers, but we always run material created with the word processor through its spell checker. It is asking for trouble to proofread yourself. Too often you read what *should* be there instead of what really *is* there. If Lotus Approach is your Windows database manager, use its spell checker. If Excel is your Mac spreadsheet, don't ignore the *toolbars*, strips of icons for common tasks. There are a dozen of them for speeding things up. Explore.

HELP FROM ALL OVER

FROM COMPUSERVE'S WORKING AT HOME FORUM

Q

I called the telco about getting a third line (i.e. fax and data). The only problem is that our subdivision does not allow any wires above ground. The telco could offer me a third line but they would have to come in with a trencher and dig a path for the third line. They asked if I would like a "bid" on the digging. That told me there were "big" bucks involved. Oh well, just another thing in the way of "home" workers.

continued...

> **A**
>
> Are you absolutely sure? Have they looked at your specific situation? I live in the same kind of subdivision and when the telco came out they found they could fish another wire through to my house for the third line.

FIVE MINUTES A DAY

Now, we know you have work to do. But you can spare five minutes a day to try something new. That's 395 minutes, or 6.58 hours, in 79 days. We found that out by bringing up Calculator over this page and punching the buttons. It's always available. Where is the separate electronic calculator when you need it? Under that stack of papers? In the kitchen? In the pocket of the jacket you wore yesterday? Both Windows and the Mac have calculators built in. You paid for one of them already.

Explore. You may find something to help you in your business that you have already bought and paid for.

KEYBOARD SHORTCUTS

A way to speed up things you already do is to learn the keyboard equivalents for the commands you often execute instead of using the mouse. When you want to print something out on either a PC running Windows or a Mac, you remove one hand from the keyboard and grab the mouse, select **File** and then select **Print**. But you can press the **Control** key, followed by **p** on a PC, or the Command (⌘) key, followed by **p** on a Macintosh. That is more efficient, and the fact that it only saves a second or two a day misses the point. Knowing the keyboard commands for things you do a lot builds confidence. With computers, that is important psychologically: there are so many things we don't know about them.

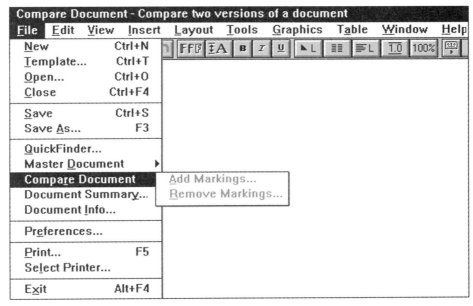

Figure 7.2 Note the keyboard shortcuts on the menus of WordPerfect for Windows.

READ ABOUT COMPUTERS

NEWSPAPER AND MAGAZINE ARTICLES

Most newspapers carry computer columns, and there are more computer magazines than anyone can imagine. If there's such a column in the newspaper you already buy, you might as well read it. Do remember that both papers and magazines are in the news business, though. You don't need a new computer every week or a new printer every month, and when you do need one it will inevitably be three months before an article comes along that will be helpful.

Figure 7.3 Newspapers cover the latest developments in the computer industry.

It is tough to decide which computer magazine to subscribe to. Some are aimed at technically sophisticated readers, others at corporate types, still others at parents or even children. At least one, *Home Office Computing*, is definitely meant for us. Look at magazines first at a newsstand or, better, in the public library. If you don't understand anything in a given magazine, put it back. If you understand everything in it, put it back too; you're supposed to learn something.

COMPUTER BOOKS

You might want a book about a program or device you already have, because you want to know more about it and because the official manuals are incomprehensible. You might also want a book about a program or device you are thinking of adding to the office, to help you decide whether or which to buy. (Don't depend too much on books for specific recommendations; the market changes faster than books.) You might buy a book to get more out of Windows or the Macintosh system. You might even want to learn more about computers, though we doubt it.

Figure 7.4 There is a computer magazine for every taste.

Computer books aren't sold just in computer shops. Regular bookstores are full of them. So full, in fact, that it is even harder to pick out one that is right for you than it is to choose a magazine.

Let's get this publisher, MIS: Press, out of the way first. It puts out the handsomest, easiest-to-understand, most exciting and up-to-date computer books in the world, as you must have noticed by now.

Figure 7.5 Books are business tools.

Seriously, the *Welcome to...* series consists of introductions to both hardware and software on which a lot of piffle has been written elsewhere. The *Teach Yourself...* books are step-by-step courses in their subjects. If you want or need to learn more about PCs, check Kris Jamsa's *Welcome to... Personal Computers*.

Most of what Larry knows about programming he knows because he read *Welcome to... Programming* by Al Stevens. It isn't Stevens' fault that not much of it stuck. We have both dipped into *Welcome to... Desktop Publishing*, by David Browne, and *Welcome to... PC Sound, Music, and MIDI*, by Tom Benford. If your business leads you in any of those directions, these books are excellent places to start.

The various *Dummies* books from IDG are worth a look, if you're not insulted by the titles, as are the *Idiot* and *Morons* (no kidding) imitations.

The Little Mac Book (Peachpit Press), by Robin Williams, is a classic. *The Little Windows Book*, by Kay Yarborough Nelson, is an easygoing introduction to that side of the fence. You don't need a computer dictionary, but if you want one anyway make it *Jargon* (Peachpit Press), also by Robin Williams with Steve Cummings.

That's it. Your interests and needs will direct you to the books that satisfy them. Or you can just learn by trial and error, like most of life.

HELP FROM ALL OVER

FROM COMPUSERVE'S WORKING AT HOME FORUM

Q

I operate 3 small businesses from my home. It is becoming increasingly difficult to keep everything separated, of course. And I am now looking into either 2 separate lines, plus an Identifying Ring service from the phone company. Or three separate lines, which seems a bit convoluted and expensive. Are there other choices? Is there a concise way to have three separate companies easily accessible over only one phone line? Is there an add-on for a home computer system that might handle this easily? And how about answering machines for each separate number? Do I really have to have three separate machines, or is there a single unit available that can handle all incoming calls? I've tried asking the local phone company, and they seem more confused than helpful. Mostly they just recommend the identifying ring service and their own Voice Mail system.

A's

I've seen answering machines which will handle 2 lines, but they couldn't take a call on both lines at the same time. Advantages to telco provided answering services is that they can answer an incoming call while you are already on the line with a client. They don't require maintenance, tapes, or break.

continued...

I found a number of very good reasons to have a dedicated voice line for my business when I started. Chief reasons:

1. My kids didn't answer the phone ever!
2. I knew when it rang that it was business.
3. No accidental extension pickups.
4. The ringer could be turned off when office hours were done.
5. Ease of separating personal and business expenses.

My key reason for choosing the telco's voicemail was that it answered when my phone was busy. The telco's central office voice mail provides me with the effect of up to 7 voice lines (seven people can try to reach me at the same time and have their message taken).

The telephone that I have has 4 voice mail boxes which I use for my own business. In the voice mail message I ask that if you are calling a certain section that you key in a certain number (#1, for example) for that part of the business. The telephone is a Panasonic Model Voice Mail EASAPHONE KXT2850.

I have purchased an answering system called "Friday" made by Bogen Communications. It allows you to have a bunch of mailboxes, each with their own mailbox message. I like it very much. It helps me separate home from business, and automates fax reception while I'm out. I got mine at Office Max. I think it was around $350. Additionally, it is all digital, so you needn't worry about those annoying little cassette tapes.

ASK QUESTIONS

COMPUTER USER GROUPS

You can also learn from other people's trials and errors. There are computer clubs, called *user groups*, practically everywhere. Some member undoubtedly will have encountered a problem similar to one you are struggling with. You can find out about user groups at the local computer store, or maybe the public library, or by buying a copy, if you can lift it, of the magazine *Computer Shopper*, which publishes a list of them every month.

GO ON-LINE

Going to meetings may not be your thing, and listening to technobabble may not be either. You don't have to leave your computer to find out what it is up to. With a modem and the proper software, it can talk to other computers and a whole lot of other people. An on-line service can bring in a flood of information, and not only about computers. On all of them, people form groups to exchange messages about whatever interests them: working at home, collecting art, building outhouses, going to movies, eating and drinking, traveling, sports, you name it. Only "building outhouses" was invented here, and that may even be true. We will never have time to explore all the on-line offerings.

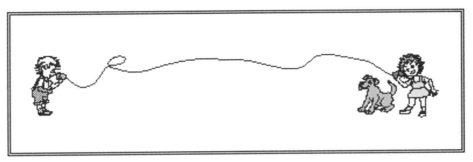

Figure 7.6 On-line communication can be fun, even addicting.

CompuServe, owned by the tax preparers H & R Block, is a major service. Wandering around it is like wandering around a big city that you've never visited before. After a while, though, you will be comfortable in it, or at least in a few familiar neighborhoods. You can get the news and weather, look things up in an encyclopedia, shop, play games or the stock market, and, most important for our purposes, exchange messages with people with similar interests. You can do all those things in any of the big on-line services, but you can do more of them—hundreds and hundreds—on CompuServe.

We got ideas for this book from the Working at Home forum on CompuServe, and so will you. To the complaint from a fellow that working out of home made him feel unprofessional, Sharon Crawford, a writer in California, replied: "My approach is that I am such a 'successful' professional, I can now have an office with windows and a view. After all, the higher you are in many companies, the less the office 'looks like an office.'"

Other samples from on-line exchanges in this chapter are from that forum. Understand, this is mail, albeit electronic mail. The people weren't speaking directly through their keyboards, although there are places where you can do that too. Also, we have edited them heavily. The longest one, which starts out with a question about fax modems and regular fax machines, went on for two or three times the length it is given here, and wandered into far more byways.

America Online is the fastest-growing service. It is easier to get around in than CompuServe, partly because its software is better and partly because there is less to get around in. The software probably is better because it started life as an Apple II and Macintosh service, although it now welcomes PCs too. Saying that there is less to get around in is purely relative. It is especially strong in on-line newspapers and magazines, *The San Jose Mercury News* and *Time* magazine for two examples, and its SeniorNet Online forum brings older people together for a wide variety of activities. When Larry explored the SeniorNet for a column in late 1993, he found generation-to-generation advice; counseling for both beginners and advanced users; exchanges on longevity and the meaning of life.

Prodigy, owned by IBM and Sears, is less useful for home business people than CompuServe or America Online. It is easy but slow to get around in. The ads can be irritating.

If CompuServe is Macy's, then America Online is Bloomingdale's. Prodigy is Sears, of course.

Those are the big three. There are also GEnie, Delphi, Bix, the Well, eWorld, and others. In addition, there are uncounted numbers of amateur bulletin boards, probably several in your neighborhood or at least area code, operated at little or no charge. You can find out about them the same way you find out about user groups: probably at a computer shop, possibly at the library, and certainly in *Computer Shopper*. That magazine runs a list of them in every issue—Alabama through Michigan one month, the rest the next month.

HELP FROM ALL OVER

FROM COMPUSERVE'S WORKING AT HOME FORUM

Q

I suspect this question has been asked 2.3k times, but I'm wondering if a Win NT machine with faxing software and a phone line can make an actual fax machine unnecessary.

A's

I like being able to fax ANYTHING on my stand-alone fax machine (insurance claim forms, etc.). However, if I had a scanner, I guess I could scan the document and then fax it from my computer. Meanwhile, since I got my fax machine BEFORE I got my fax/modem, I use that 99% of the time.

Exactly what I do. Works perfectly well.

Q

Do you find that most text-type docs scan "perfectly," or do you have to make adjustments?

continued...

A's

Usually perfectly. I can frequently tweak a very poor original so that the output is *better* (more legible) than the original. I have an HP Scanjet IIcx. It's certainly overkill for my purposes most of the time. (I use the color capabilities to scan in pictures of my friends' kids and make Windows wallpaper for them!)

In addition to what's already been said about being able to FAX forms, signatures, and so forth and not wanting to buy a scanner just for that, I'll add that I like being able to jump up and send a FAX anytime, without having to quit some other program on my computer just so I can run a FAX program. Likewise, my stand-alone FAX machine can receive FAXes even if I'm using my computer for something else— or even if I've got my computer turned off.

You obviously are not a Windows user! The question asked whether a solution was acceptable with Windows NT. With Windows fax software you don't "leave your program to fax": you print your document normally but to a fax modem. It takes only slightly longer than printing it normally and it's automatic. Windows fax software receives faxes automatically, in the background, while you're running other software without interruption. The definite limitation to a computerized fax solution: The computer must be on.

I'm a Windows user. I'm just not a Windows admirer. By the way, I probably should have said this explicitly and I'll do it now: I'm not saying that a FAX modem plus Windows is a bad thing. I'm merely describing why *I* don't generally do things that way; people in other circumstances or with different needs may be very happy with that configuration. For the things *I* do with my computer and the kind of FAX traffic *I* have, *my* experience was that the FAX modem was more trouble than it was worth—and all this technology stuff is here to save me time, not create more problems for me to work around!

I have an old PC with Windows 3.11, a fax modem, WinFax Pro from Delrina, and no fax machine. It has replaced the need for a fax machine, for me, by 99%. If I added a scanner it would be 100%. However, rarely—but every now and then—I do need to be able to fax something that is not in the computer. A scanner would solve that problem. Also, the computer has to be left on 24 hours a day in order to receive faxes.

One environmentally friendly advantage you didn't mention: you can look at a fax before you print it. In this way, "junk faxes" get deleted, not printed.

Fax filtering is wonderful. I can't even begin to count the reams of papers that have been saved by deleting Junk advertising faxes without wasting paper!

Isn't that bad for the computer, even if your monitor is turned off? Doesn't it ever need a "break?" Wouldn't this shorten the life of the unit?

Some argue that you have more chance of equipment failure from surges at startup (plus the heating and contracting of electronic components). The hard drives today are rated for 100,000 hours mean time between failures. That's about eleven years, which should be long enough. You DO use more electricity, of course.

Yeah, let's see 5 kwatt/hour. It costs me about 25 cents to run a 100-watt light bulb for 24 hours. So I guess I'm spending pennies to leave my computer on at night, so it can automate tasks during the overnight. Compare that with the cost of lost productivity during your work day!

Turning on and off a desktop computer is actually quite a harsh and shocking experience for it… kind of waking up in the morning over and over again.

THE INFORMATION SUPERHIGHWAY

Then there is the Internet. Unless you've been locked in the bathroom the last year or two, you've heard about the Internet. It is a loose collection of nobody-knows-how-many-million people and nobody-knows-how-many-thousand computers all over the world. We can guarantee you that there are things on the Internet that will help you run your business. We can also guarantee you that you don't have the time to find them. Unless you are one of the lucky people who have a free connection to the Internet through a corporation, university, or something, you don't have the money to find them either. Someday, maybe.

Figure 7.7 Building a CD-ROM library.

Don't let that CD-ROM drive go to waste either. With Microsoft's Bookshelf in it, you can have a complete reference library—dictionary, thesaurus, encyclopedia, atlas, and that's not all—right at hand. There is much more available in the exploding CD-ROM market, and a sample is discussed in Chapter 5.

Figure 7.8 Good luck. May you live in interesting times.

PERIPHERALS

Getting Your Feet Wet In a Sea Called Internet

"The government always discovers a technology after its moment is passing," the economist and author George Gilder says in an interview in the September/October issue of Wired. "It's not going to change with Clinton and Gore. The dog technologies run to Washington, decked out like poodles. The politician is always the dog's best friend."

One of the technologies Vice President Al Gore is pushing is the information superhighway, which will link everyone at home or office to everything else — movies and television shows, shopping services, electronic mail and huge collections of data — starting perhaps with the elaborate structure envisioned by Bell Atlantic and Tele-Communications. But the Internet, already linking 10 million to 15 million people in a version of the data superhighway (albeit without movies and shopping), shows, in Mr. Gilder's words, that "to have a very rich fabric of services you don't need a regimented system of control."

No one is in charge of the Internet. You do not visit a retail outlet to buy the sign-up software or fill out a card that flutters out of a magazine. Yet the Internet, which grew out of a 1969 Department of Defense contract to connect university, military and defense contractors, keeps growing; no one really knows how much or how fast. Paul Gilster, in "The Internet Navigator: The Essential Guide to Network Exploration for the Individual Dial-Up User" (John Wiley & Sons), writes that by 1985, "approximately 100 networks formed the Internet."

continued...

He continues: "By 1989, that number had risen to 500. The Network Information Center of the Defense Data Network Information Center found 2,218 networks connected as of January 1990. By June 1991, the National Science Foundation Network Information Center pegged it at close to 4,000, and connections have more than doubled within the last two years. If we extrapolate based on current numbers, the Internet could reach 40 million people by 1995, 100 million by 1998. Its current growth rate is 15 percent monthly."

Most individual users have formal or informal connections to a network linked to the Internet. "Formal" means working for or attending a member company or university; "informal" means having worked for a member or being able to ingratiate oneself with a strategically placed officer. Michael Fraase, in his breezy "The Mac Internet Tour Guide" (Ventana Press), devotes four sections to general instructions "about who to befriend and what arcane terms to utter so you'll sound like a seasoned expert." Commercial on-line services like Compuserve, America Online and Delphi have begun to add Internet links, some limited to sending and receiving electronic mail, others with full service. A host of so-called service providers, providing gateways to the Internet, have also sprung up—probably three or four hosts if you do not read this first thing in the morning.

Connecting a business to the Internet can cost thousands of dollars, depending on its size; an individual without a real or feigned relationship to a member organization can seek a service provider. Rates are reasonable, considering what the money buys.

Without even trying, I have gathered eight new or recently updated books on the Internet. With, say, MCI Mail or

Prodigy, you can learn as you go along. The Internet not only deserves preparation, it absolutely demands it. One reason is that, as noted, nobody is in charge. Another is that the Internet prefers to speak UNIX, an unfriendly language in which your address might be "hildyj.chi.il.us." You can get by, as you can in most other foreign countries, by speaking English and learning the UNIX equivalent of "Where is the bathroom, please?" and a few other stock lines. But to be completely comfortable, you will have to be able to say, in UNIX, "It seems to me and to most of my peers, epistemologically speaking, that Forster is flaccid." Ordinary people will applaud Windows and Macintosh software.

"Internet: Getting Started" (PTR Prentice Hall), edited by April Marine, Susan Kirkpatrick and Vivian Neou, and "Internet: Mailing Lists" (PTR Prentice Hall), edited by Edward T. L. Hardie and Vivian Neou, have been updated. "The Internet Guide for New Users" (McGraw-Hill), by Daniel P. Dern, goes into more detail than the books already mentioned, which can be viewed as an advantage or not. Mr. Dern is also the editor of a new bimonthly magazine, Internet World. "Navigating the Internet" (Sams), by Mark Gibbs and Richard J. Smith, also gains, or loses, points for comprehensiveness. O'Reilly & Associates of Sebastopol, Calif., publishes both a slim and a fat volume. "Connecting to the Internet,"by Susan Estrada, is the first; "The Whole Internet User's Guide and Catalog," by Ed Krol, is the second.

From the Peripherals column, Oct. 26, 1993. Copyright © 1993 by The New York Times Company. Reprinted by permission.

REMINDER LIST:

- Look at the programs you already have. There are pleasant surprises in them. The more you know about your programs, the better you can conduct your business.
- Keep in touch with developments through magazines and books.
- Ask for help, either in person or on-line.

THE REST OF
YOUR LIFE

TO DO LIST

- ✓ There's nothing here you have to do
- ✓ There are lots of things you might want to try

Nobody works all the time. Even you. It just seems that way sometimes. You watch television, jog, sip a Scotch, play squash or tennis, go to the movies, do other things we'd rather not mention. Meanwhile, that computer up in the spare bedroom is idle, its mouse unpetted, its CD-ROM drive pining away. It never has any fun. It's not supposed to. But you can have fun with it.

HOBBIES

There are programs for cooks, bartenders, gardeners, musicians, and fans of all kinds of sports. You can play golf on a computer or play golf at a course and analyze your game on the computer afterward. There are even programs to pick a winning lottery number. Sure. If you believe a computer can do that, why aren't there a bunch of rich computers lazing around on a sunny beach?

Figure 8.1 There are computer programs for almost every hobby imaginable.

TRACING YOUR ROOTS

If your ancestors came over on the *Mayflower* you probably already know that. If they met the boat you probably don't. But even without royal or historic hopes, genealogy has attracted many people for many years. One friend of ours traced his family back to the early 19th century, but then he found that his late 19th-century grandfather had been adopted, meaning that he had been tracing the wrong family tree from gramps on back. Another friend admitted that his family tree was probably too dull and certainly too hard to trace, so he tracked his wife's instead. Genealogy can be tedious work, what with searching old records, writing letters to possible lost relatives, plodding through ancient graveyards. But there is an undeniable interest in what amounts to looking for yourself. Computers make the job easier.

There is a wealth of genealogical programs, several of which are shareware. We have looked at Family Ties for Windows from Individual Software of Pleasanton, CA, and Family Tree Maker Deluxe CD-ROM edition from Banner Blue Software of Fremont, CA.

With Family Tree Maker, you enter the names, birth dates, birthplaces, and marriage date and place of yourself and spouse, and the names, sex, and birth dates of your children in a form on the screen. Then you enter information for both sets of parents and each of your children. Information is typed in only once. For example, the form for your parents already has your name, sex, and birth date entered, because you typed it into the first form. There are numerous other forms—including ones for anecdotes.

As you gather information about your ancestors, you enter it into the forms provided and, as you progress, print it out, either as duplicates of the on-screen forms or automatically as family-tree charts that look something like business flow charts. Family Tree Maker offers a start in research as well. The CD-ROM contains listings of family pedigrees, Social Security records, and other documents.

Eventually, however, you will have to go to the original records, either on paper or on disks. Disks are much easier to search than printed documents. Programs like these are not going to spare you from dank graveyards or danker halls of records, but they make it far easier to organize the information you gather through dogged investigative reporting. Family Ties for Windows is simpler, with forms, tabs, and icons. As with Family Tree Maker, you only have to enter the information once for it to appear on other forms or on the printouts. Family Ties handles the Gedcom (Genealogical Data Communications) format developed by the family history department of the Church of Jesus Christ of Latter-Day Saints, a rich source of information even for non-Mormons.

COMPUTER ART

Always yearned to be an artist? You can paint on a computer. We don't mean smearing burnt sienna on the screen, we mean drawing with the mouse or, if you are really committed, with a stylus on a tablet, where the shapes you draw are translated into images on the screen. There are big programs, CorelDRAW for example, which can do almost anything, and little programs, like Claris Brushstrokes and Fractal Design's Dabbler, which can probably do as much or more than you require.

With Paintbrush, you can do primitives, like the original Grandma Shannon on the facing page. If you use a PC, you already have Paintbrush among the Windows Accessories.

You don't have to be able to draw a straight line; these programs do it for you. Or a square, a circle, a curve. They can sharpen or soften the image, splatter it with drops, make the screen imitate canvas or rough paper. You might not care to take a PowerMac with 21-inch monitor out for Sunday painting, but you can make a sketch on real paper at the wharf or in the woods and bring it back to the computer to elaborate it. With a stylus you can trace the sketch directly into the program, or with a scanner you can transfer it in.

Figure 8.2 Computer art can be as intricate as you like depending on your imagination.

THE REFERENCE SHELF

You are never going to read the latest Danielle Steele or Michael Crichton on a computer. You can take a subportable to bed with you, but we bet you don't. Who wants to curl up with a cozy computer on a chilly night? You could even carry one into the bathroom, instead of Reader's Digest, but who would?

Reference books, which you don't read through, are another thing. A complete reference library on CD-ROM fits in a few inches of space. Microsoft makes many of the leading, and often the best, ones. You can find standards like encyclopedias, dictionaries, and thesauruses, or reference disks on such specific topics as health and medicine, programming, wine, and warplanes.

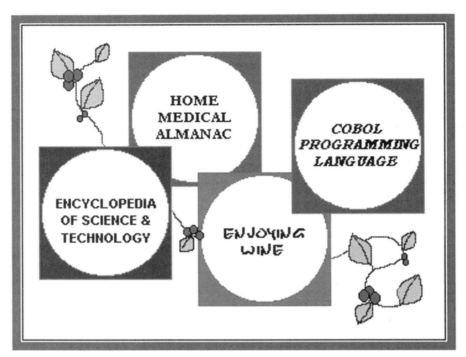

Figure 8.3 Many reference materials are available on CD-ROM.

ENCYCLOPEDIAS

Among encyclopedias, we like Microsoft's Encarta best, but there are also Grolier, Infopedia, and others. Let us try, by way of example, a search in Encarta. Click on the **Contents** button on the menu bar, and type the word **Shannon**. (We know you wouldn't type that word, but we are rather fond of it.) A longish paragraph on the river—354 kilometers or about 220 miles long—appears.

There is no Shannon in the Gallery, another menu item, but there is a listing for the 1906 San Francisco earthquake. Since that is Larry's home town, he calls it up and sees a black-and-white photograph of ruins and fire, with a brief summarizing caption.

Back to the original subject. Selecting **Atlas** brings a globe of the world to the screen, with instructions to click on arrows to spin the globe and then to click on the desired spot. Clicking on **Ireland** brings a legend that says Northern Europe, and there is a zoom-in button for a closer view. Clicking on that brings a map from Jan Mayen Island in the far north to Czechslovakia in the south. What in the world is Jan Mayen? The name is pronounced through the speakers in what sounds like an authentic accent. Clicking on **Go to Topic** produces a paragraph on the Norwegian island discovered in 1607 by Henry Hudson.

Well, we live 20 miles from the Hudson River, so we switch to the **Category Browser**, then **Exploration and Explorers**, then to **Hudson** himself, a longish article and a portrait. The advantage with a reference work on CD-ROM rather than in print is that it is so easy to wander and digress... if that can be called an advantage.

DICTIONARIES

Random House has an unabridged dictionary on disk, in a text-only version that works in either PCs or Macintoshes, and another with sound and graphics for PCs. Truly committed word lovers will want the *Oxford English Dictionary* on disk, but at around $900 it is too pricy for most of us.

SIX-IN-ONE

A complete reference library on one disk is Microsoft Bookshelf, with a dictionary, thesaurus, encyclopedia, world atlas, book of quotations, and the World Almanac. That should take care of most common questions, such as bringing up a map of the southeastern United States if you can't remember which states Alabama is between (Mississippi and Georgia); another word for alcoholism (dipsomania); the weight of the Statue of Liberty (225 tons); or an apt quotation for a presentation at the women's club: *"I've tried several varieties of sex," Tallulah Bankhead said. "The conventional position makes me claustrophobic and the others give me a stiff neck or lockjaw."* Well, better keep looking.

"Business? it's quite simple: it's other people's money." That's Dumas. And that's another example of how you can get lost in a CD-ROM.

TRAVEL

The best way to plan a trip is to find a trustworthy travel agent and let her do it for you. (Jan is a travel agent. She insisted on that sentence.) But some people get as much fun, maybe even more, out of planning a trip as in taking one.

Figure 8.4 Let your computer help plan your vacation.

Plenty of map programs are available. With some, like Automap, you can plan your route on color maps and find out about interstate highways and back roads, major attractions, things to see and do in big cities and rural areas, where to find RV parks, and stuff like that. Other map programs give you information about foreign countries.

On any of the main on-line services, there are travel groups where you can get other people's advice about destinations, in return for your own experiences, and even plot out flights and make reservations.

Workaholics or playaholics with a portable computer can take it along on a vacation, playing Tetris or writing business letters 35,000 feet above the Great Plains, or picking up e-mail at the Marriott. If you do take a computer aboard, don't worry about the gateway metal detector zapping it—the dangers are slight—but do be prepared to open it and turn it on to prove that it is a computer and not some other fiendish device. That means keeping a charge in the battery so you don't have to look for an electric outlet. Also, be aware that the airlines have rules about using computers on board. Usually they must be put away during take-off and landing.

OTHER PROGRAMS

There are programs that give legal advice, make a business plan, and teach foreign languages, math, and science. Others help you make repairs around the house or apartment, build a house from scratch, landscape a yard, do magic tricks, start your own computer bulletin board (forget it!), learn to play bridge or a keyboard, just about anything you can think of. Publishers big and small are making new entries and killing old ones every day.

A catalog on CD-ROM arrived here a month before Christmas with merchandise offerings from 21 national retailers—Land's End, the Metropolitan Museum of Art, and Sony Music among them—which you could browse through on the screen and order gifts, through your modem if you wish. It was the first we've seen, but it surely will not be the last.

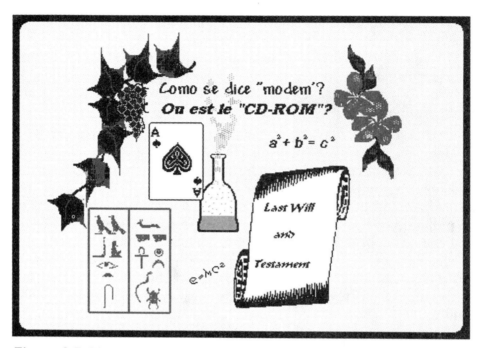

Figure 8.5 There are computer programs that teach almost anything under the sun. It's like going back to school without leaving your home.

THE KIDS

Suppose that home-office computer belongs to a child or children evenings and weekends. Rules must be set. Kid Desk for young children, or At Ease for old ones, both mentioned in Chapter 5, may help if your computer is a double-duty machine. But with or without such programs, your business files must be protected. The best means of protection are frequent backups, and certainly at the end of the work week insofar as the home work week ever ends. But one Friday afternoon you say, "the hell with it, I'm tired," and the next morning is the Saturday that Amanda wipes out Accounts Receivable or The Manhole discombobulates the CD-ROM drive. (The Manhole, from Cyan, is an outstanding game that any child who can operate a mouse can explore.)

Figure 8.6 The Manhole is fun and easy to master.

ABCS

Aside from games, which the children can pick better than we can, there are standard applications intended for youngsters: word processors, spreadsheets, graphics programs. The Children's Writing Center, from The Learning Company of Fremont, CA, processes words, of course, but it also lets the child add graphics and text boxes, check spelling and find synonyms, lay out good-looking pages, design letterheads, and much more.

The Cruncher, from Davidson & Associates of Torrance, CA, teaches mathematical fundamentals through an electronic spreadsheet that remains a handy and attractive tool after the lessons are learned. With tutorials, projects, templates, charting and graphing, and trigonometry functions, The Cruncher may be all the spreadsheet you need.

Using Kid CAD, a 3-D building kit from Davidson, a child can build structures on the screen, furnish and populate them, paint them, examine them from many angles, and (often the best part) destroy them.

These programs come and go, and there is no substitute for shopping around, either in person or in the pages of mail-order catalogues. There are shelves of educational programs, often called "edutainment" because it is hard to say whether *edu* or *tainment* is more important.

Another consideration is whether children, particularly older ones, will look down on a children's program. Only you know, where your kids are concerned, and probably you don't know either. If Charlie insists on doing his homework with Microsoft Word or Ami Pro, don't fight it. Let him try. In a few weeks he may well offer you tips. "Oh, dad. **Select All** with **Command-A**, not the mouse." Maybe he will take over Word, and you will switch to the Children's Writing Center.

THE KID IN YOU

Games are not just for kids. Maxis, the publisher of the addictive SimCity, reports that 75 percent of its players are over the age of 18. And there is edutainment for adults, too, such as Wrath of the Gods from Luminaria, which, with its sparkling graphics, makes you want to explore Greek mythology. Don't take it too seriously, though. The ancient Greeks didn't have an ATM in their Hades.

We, being old-fashioned, prefer solitaire, which is far more fun to play on a computer than on the dining-room table with a real deck of cards. There are a number of excellent solitaire variations in the Microsoft Entertainment Packs for Windows machines. Other companies also publish solitaire programs. The best by far, in this office's opinion, is Solitaire Antics from Ant Software for both Windows and the Mac. There are 22 games, from pretty easy to damned hard, as well as animations and sound effects that are fun at first but that you will probably turn off after a while.

Figure 8.7 Kids of all ages can enjoy computer games.

COMPUTER GAMES GROW UP

A good example of the evolution of computer games is Zork. Zork harks back to early adventure games, which existed before the personal computer was invented. They were pure prose. A sentence appeared on the screen and the player typed a simple sentence in response, usually just a verb and a noun in the early days (**go west**). Through these means, you explored a world on the screen and in your head, fought monsters, found tools and treasure, eventually succeeding or failing to master an imaginary universe. The prose Zorks, all six of them, have recently been reissued by the publisher, Infocom, and they are still fun and challenging. But they are by way of a promotion for Return to Zork, a CD-ROM with real actors playing the parts in video clips, animations, sound—a modern epic. Your kids might not have the patience to play a prose Zork; you might not have the skills to play Return to Zork.

FROM THE ORIGINAL ZORK

```
You are facing the north side of a white house. There is
no door here, and all the windows are boarded up. To the
north a narrow path winds through the trees.
```

>walk around house

```
Behind House
You are behind the white house. A path leads into the for-
est to the east. In one corner of the house there is a
small window which is slightly ajar.
```

>open window

```
With great effort, you open the window far enough to allow
entry.
```

>enter

```
Kitchen
You are in the kitchen of the white house. A table seems
to have been used recently for the preparation of food. A
passage leads to the west and a dark staircase can be seen
leading upward. A dark chimney leads down and to the east
is a small window which is open.
On the table is an elongated brown sack, smelling of hot
peppers.
A bottle is sitting on the table.
```

```
The glass bottle contains:
  A quantity of water
```

>take bottle

```
Taken.
```

>take sack

```
Taken.
```

>inventory
```
You are carrying:
  A brown sack
  A glass bottle
  The glass bottle contains:
    A quantity of water
  A leaflet
```

Pretty tame stuff by 1995 standards. Today the Zork game is more like an adventure movie with you as the star.

SCREEN SAVERS

Screen savers have evolved too. With early monitors, there was a danger that an image left unchanging on the screen for too long would impress itself on the phosphors and become permanent. So the screen saver would blank the screen or put a simple moving image on it, if things were idle for a certain length of time. It has been years since we've heard of an image burning into a screen, but screen savers have developed into a major category. You don't need one. You will get one. After Dark, from Berkeley Systems, is ours. You can find it everywhere, for both PCs and Macs.

REMINDER LIST

- Have fun!

KEYBOARD SHORTCUTS

Most programs that require a mouse have keyboard alternatives—shortcuts—that let you keep your hand on the keys. Here are a few for your system software that you might find helpful. Keyboard shortcuts can be time saving, but keeping your fingers on the keyboard all the time can be bad for your health.

MICROSOFT WINDOWS

On the menu bar, note that the first letters of the world <u>F</u>ile, <u>W</u>indow, <u>O</u>ption and <u>H</u>elp are underlined. That is to remind you that these letters may be used with the **Alt** key to open the menu.

Alt + F	opens the file menu
Alt + W	opens the window menu
Alt + O	opens the option menu
Alt + H	opens the help menu

Within those menus, keyboard shortcuts are listed to the right of the operation you want to perform.

F7	to move a highlighted program item (icon) from one group to another
Del	to delete a highlighted program item
F8	to copy a highlighted program item from one group to another

These can be handy if you need to make changes in your programs or if you use the same program in a number of ways, for instance, if you want to have your graphics program available for use with both a word processor and a spreadsheet.

MACINTOSH

The command key is the one with a cloverleaf ⌘ on it and, if the keyboard is an Apple one, an apple.

⌘ + N	opens a new file
⌘ + O	opens an existing file
⌘ + P	prints file
⌘ + W	closes file
⌘ + Z	undo

⌘ + X	cut
⌘ + C	copy
⌘ + V	paste
⌘ + A	select all
⌘ + F	find/change
⌘ + G	find again
⌘ + Y	ejects highlighted disk

Most Macintosh keyboard shortcuts are the same within programs on the Mac, as well.

OTHER PROGRAMS

To find keyboard shortcuts within other programs, pull down a menu using your mouse. If there is a shortcut, it should be listed on the right side of the menu opposite the function it performs.

RECOMMENDED HARDWARE

COMPUTER SYSTEMS

The products mentioned in the main text are ones that we are either personally acquainted with or that we know set the standard in their categories. There are other, but not many other, products that are as good or better. The mechanical differences between, say, a $3000 system and a $2000 system may not matter to the home-office worker who has not been seduced by technology, but the stability of a company, the support it offers, and the warranty and service policy should.

PCs

- Compaq
- IBM

Macintoshes

- Macintosh Quadra
- PowerMac

Portable Computers

- Macintosh PowerBook
- Toshiba PC

PRINTERS

For PCs

- Epson dot-matrix printers
- Hewlett-Packard laser printers

For Macintoshes

- Apple StyleWriter
- Apple LaserWriter

MODEMS

- Hayes
- U.S. Robotics
- Zoom

CD-ROM DRIVES

- NEC
- Toshiba

SOUND CARDS

- Sound Blaster
- Media Vision
- Turtle Beach

EXTERNAL HARD DRIVES

- SyQuest
- Bernoulli boxes

SCANNERS

- Canon
- Metrotech

TAPE BACKUPS

- Colorado Memory Systems

RECOMMENDED SOFTWARE

RECOMMENDED PC SOFTWARE

As with hardware, the software products mentioned in the main text are ones that we use or have tried or that we know are good from other people's reports. Saving money on software can be very expensive in the long run.

WORD PROCESSORS

- Ami Pro for Windows
- Microsoft Word for Windows
- WordPerfect for Windows
- Q&A Write
- Accent (foreign language word processor)

SPREADSHEETS

- Borland Quattro Pro
- Lotus 1-2-3
- Microsoft Excel

DATABASES

- Borland Paradox
- FileMaker Pro
- Lotus Approach

INTEGRATED PROGRAMS

- ClarisWorks
- Microsoft Works
- PFS:WindowsWorks

DESKTOP PUBLISHING AND GRAPHICS

Publishing

- Microsoft Publisher
- The Print Shop
- PFS:Publisher

Graphics

- Aldus FreeHand
- CorelDRAW
- Paintbrush

Presentations

- Harvard Graphics
- Microsoft PowerPoint

ON-LINE SERVICES

- America Online
- CompuServe
- Prodigy

COMMUNICATIONS SOFTWARE FOR THE MODEM

- Crosstalk
- Hayes Smartcom
- Procomm Plus

UTILITIES PROGRAMS

- Norton Desktop
- Norton Utilities
- PC Tools

BUSINESS APPLICATIONS

Sample Letters

- Professional Letterworks
- Sales LetterWorks

Promotion

- Publicity Builder

Mailing and Other Specialized Programs

- MySoftware

Personal Information Manager

- Lotus Organizer

Personal Finances

- Quicken

Protecting Your Work

- KidDesk

RECOMMENDED MACINTOSH SOFTWARE

WORD PROCESSORS

- MacWrite Pro
- Microsoft Word
- WordPerfect
- WriteNow

SPREADSHEETS

- Lotus 1-2-3
- Microsoft Excel

DATABASES

- Claris FileMaker Pro

INTEGRATED PROGRAMS

- ClarisWorks
- Microsoft Works

COMMUNICATIONS PROGRAMS

- SitComm
- White Knight

RECOMMENDED CD-ROMS

ENCYCLOPEDIAS

- Encarta
- Grolier
- Infopedia

DICTIONARY

- Random House Unabridged

MICROSOFT BOOKSHELF

contains:

- Dictionary
- Thesaurus
- Encyclopedia
- Atlas
- Quotations
- Almanac

RECOMMENDED BOOKS AND MAGAZINES

BOOKS

These books are intended to be good places to start.

Welcome to... Personal Computers, by Kris Jamsa, MIS:Press

Welcome to... Desktop Publishing, by David Browne, MIS:Press

Welcome to... PC Sound, Music, and MIDI, by Tom Benford, MIS:Press

Welcome to... Programming, by Al Stevens, MIS:Press

The Little Mac Book, by Robin Williams, Peachpit Press

The Little Windows Book, by Kay Yarborough Nelson, Peachpit Press

Jargon, by Robin Williams with Steve Cummings, Peachpit Press

DOS for Dummies, by Dan Gookin, IDG Books

MAGAZINES

These, too, are good places to start and to help you stay smart.

GENERAL

- *Home Office Computing*
- *Computer Shopper*

SPECIALIZED

- *PC Computing*
- *PC Magazine*
- *MacUser*
- *MacWorld*

HISTORY

HISTORY SCHMISTORY

The word "computer" goes back to the 1600's. It referred to a person who computed, at first with paper and pen or pencil, later with adding machines. Here is how we got from brains and beads on wires to brains and silicon.

In a book on personal computers written in the Dark Ages of the early 1980's, Phil Bertoni called the new machine "an abacus on amphetamines." That's good, and it also tells us how long people have been trying to substitute mechanical power for brawn and brains.

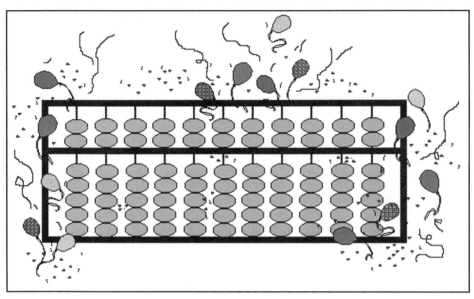

Figure E.1 An abacus on amphetamines.

Don't imagine that Roman children memorized the VIII times multiplication table, the way we memorized the 8 times table. If they needed to do arithmetic in adult life, they used an abacus, as some of the world still does.

In 1642, the French philosopher Pascal built a mechanical adding machine. Some 30 years later the German philosopher Leibniz improved it so it could multiply. Pascal got a computer programming language named after him. Poor Leibniz didn't.

The next step came from an unlikely source, the loom. Joseph Marie Jacquard (1752 to 1834) devised perforated boards, reminiscent of those punch cards that used to come with your bills, so his workers could weave complex patterns without a great deal of craftsmanship.

When the 1880 census in the growing United States took too many years to compile, Herman Hollerith combined Jacquard's idea—perforated cards rather than boards—with the newish electrical technology and devised a way to speed the counting of the 1890 census.

Earlier in the 19th century, an eccentric English genius named Charles Babbage had invented what for all practical purposes was the modern digital computer, but he never actually got one built. In association with Augusta Ada Byron, he worked out the basic principles of input, storage (now usually called memory), processing, and output of the machine that is on a million desks today. His partner, Lady Lovelace, got a programming language, Ada, named after her. Poor Babbage didn't.

Through the first decades of the 20th century, analog computers were built for specialized jobs. (A watch with hands is analog; a watch with numbers on a little screen is digital.) The slide rule, now dead but once as much the mark of a serious number cruncher as a tool belt is the mark of a professional electrician or carpenter, was an analog device.

The beginnings of the digital computer, in the 1940's, are somewhat confused and controversial. There is no doubt, however, that the idea of storing the program (instructions) in the computer, rather than rewiring the machine for each new problem, was that of John von Neuman, a Hungarian-American. That is why your computer is just a box of widgets until you load a program into its memory, when it becomes a box of widgets you can write with, calculate with, draw pictures with, play games with.

The first all-electronic computer was Eniac (Electronic Numerical Integrator and Computer), built in 1946. It contained vacuum tubes, which older readers may remember, 18,000 of them, requiring much electricity, creating much heat, and failing much too often. But it could calculate like nothing before it could calculate, about as well and as fast as a handheld calculator you can buy for a few dollars today.

Then, in the 1950's, came the transistor, which replaced the power-hungry and fragile tube, and, in the 1960's, the integrated circuit, which put a lot of transistors on one silicon wafer. Over the years, the silicon wafers, usually called chips, have gone from holding a few thousand transistors to more than a million. That is why you have more computing power on your desk today than the

Pentagon had in its basement when the French lost their war in Vietnam at Dienbienphu.

There are four categories of computers, with the lines between them increasingly blurred. The personal computer, which we are concerned with, is sometimes called the microcomputer. Next, the workstation, for heavy-duty office work and intensive tasks like engineering; the minicomputer, for laboratories and bigger businesses or departments, and the mainframe, for major government agencies, financial institutions, and such. Within the mainframe category is the supercomputer, the swift and vastly expensive machine that can calculate the size of the universe, or even your Visa bill, in seconds.

The lines are blurred because today's personal computer is yesterday's workstation, the day before yesterday's minicomputer, and the day before that's mainframe. Many businesses find it more efficient, and cheaper, for workers to sit at high-level personal computers, tied together in a network, than to seat them at terminals, which are hardly more than keyboards and monitors, tied to minicomputers or mainframes.

The first microcomputer, the Altair, was offered as a $400 kit in 1974. The demand for it overwhelmed the small company, MITS, that built it. Or to be more accurate, didn't build it; it was a kit, after all, and the buyer had to actually put the thing together. When, or if, successfully completed, it couldn't do any work, but it was a computer—good Lord, a real computer—on the kitchen table or workbench. The Altair and its competitors attracted dyed-in-the-wool techies, to get back to looms. But toward the end of the 70's other companies sensed the potential, and Radio Shack and others offered premanufactured computers that could actually do something, and two kids, Steve Wozniak and Steve Jobs, started Apple. Their Apple II computers, in a variety of models, are no longer manufactured but are still around. IBM offered its first PC in 1981, just to pick up a few bucks in what it didn't see as an important market, and Apple introduced the Macintosh in 1984. Although the first

Mac was ridiculously underpowered, it represented the mouse-and-icon future.

Earlier kinds of machines unemployed physical workers. The Jacquard loom put many weavers out of work. The railroad put stagecoach drivers out of work. The threshing machine and motorized plow put farmhands out of work. In the publishing industry, the computer, and related inventions, put printers out of work. For many of us, the VCR made the movie theater an occasional treat rather than a regular part of the routine. If you have a fax machine, you seldom need a messenger on a bicycle. If you have a modem, you don't need the mail for ordinary documents.

But the new technology is doing something almost unheard of in the past. If you store your documents on a hard disk, you don't need a filing clerk. An electronic mailing list, and word processing, can let one secretary do the job of many. Programmed buying and selling of stocks replaces dozens of people on the floor of the exchange. The jackhammer took the jobs of a lot of guys with picks. Will the computer replace the thousands of people who figured their pay, kept the accounts, and managed those who did those jobs?

It sure looks like it. In a home office, you both benefit and suffer from a revolution in the way most work will get done in the new millenium.

GLOSSARY

We have not hesitated to adapt or just plain copy definitions from the main text.

Applications Software

Software that performs a specific function, such as word processing or database management.

Audio Board

A circuit card (that's a board) that plays audio (that's sound).

Back-up

Copies on floppy or hard disks or tape of the work stored on your main hard disk.

Baud Rate

As generally used, the number of bits a computer will send through the modem each second. The higher the baud rate the better.

Bays

Spaces inside the main box in which accessory circuit boards are attached to the motherboard that you can get to from the outside.

Bit

The smallest unit of data. A bit, short for binary digit, is usually thought of as being either a 1 or a 0, because we can do arithmetic with 1s and 0s. If we were doing logic with bits, we would think of them as "true/false." In other contexts, they might be "either/or," "yes/no," "male/female," or "Republican/Democrat." Computers reduce the whole complicated world to "1/0."

Bit-mapped Fonts

Characters drawn in a pattern of dots. Bit-mapped Times Roman, 24-point, bold is one drawing and Times Roman, 12-point, bold is another drawing. Bit-mapped fonts adhere to the traditional definition of "font." (They can be changed in limited and mostly ugly ways.)

Boot, Cold Boot, Warm Boot

To boot a computer is to start it. A cold boot is turning the power switch from "off" to "on." A warm boot is restarting the computer without turning it off first.

BPS

Bits per second. The speed at which a modem sends or receives data.

Byte

Eight bits. A byte stores a letter, number, or other character or command. A capital "A" is 01000001, a carriage return is 00001101. Everything in a document, even a space (00100001), is at least one byte.

Card

Also called a board, a flattish piece of something or another with circuits, chips, and other electrical gizmos on it. It fits into a *slot* or *bay*.

CD-ROM

Acronym for Compact Disk-Read Only Memory. CD-ROM disks store much more information than floppy disks or ordinary hard disks, but the information can't be changed.

Clip Art

Drawings or other graphics you can take from a program or collection and place in your own reports or presentations. Clip art used to be on paper—hence it was "clipped"— although the kind we are concerned with here is on disk.

CPS

Characters per second.

CPU

Central Processing Unit, the chip inside the system box that does the work. PCs operate with CPUs made by Intel, for the most part, and the Pentium and 80486 are the important ones now. Macs operate with CPUs made by Motorola. The 68030 and 68040 were important the day before yesterday; PowerPC chips with a variety of numbers are important now.

Crash

When your hard disk goes blooey. This can happen if the head that stores and retrieves data comes into actual contact with the disk's surface and grinds its protective coating, or it can be caused by a virus.

The term "crash" is also used for other disasters. Crashes are why you back up regularly. Everything and everybody crashes eventually.

CRT

Cathode ray tube. The monitor's screen is the front of the CRT.

Cursor

The blinking dot or line or arrow or whatever that shows you where you are working in a file.

Cursor Movement Keys

The arrow keys on the keyboard that allow you to move your cursor without grabbing the mouse.

Database

An organized collection of information like a telephone or little black book.

Database Manager

A program to manage and manipulate the information stored in a database.

Density

A measure of the amount of information that can be stored in a fixed area. Floppy disks are sold in various densities. Buy the highest-density disks your computer can handle.

Desktop Publishing

Creating professional-looking flyers, newsletters and other documents on your computer rather than going out to a print shop.

Directory

A list of related files on a hard disk.

DOS

Disk Operating System. The basic system that makes a PC work. MS-DOS, by far the most common operating system, is made by Microsoft.

Dot Pitch

The spacing of the dots on the monitor. Closer is better.

Drawing Program

A graphics program that stores the pieces of a drawing as mathematical formulas.

ELF

Extremely low frequency.

E-Mail

Electronic mail. Letters, except that you don't drop them into a mailbox.

Expansion Slot

A space inside the computer where you can insert an additional card.

Extended Memory

Memory above one megabyte.

Expanded Memory

An early, tricky scheme to access more memory than DOS computers could handle. On the way out.

File

A collection of information you have given a name and stored on a disk.

Flat File Database

A database manager that stores its information in one table. In a client list, the blanks that you fill in with a name, address, and other information are called fields, and all the fields for that client are in one record in one table.

Font

In traditional typography, a font is a given name, size, and style of type. Times Roman, 24-point, bold is one font; Time Roman, 12-point, bold is a different font, as is Times Roman, 12-point, condensed. In computerized typography, the definition of a font often does not include its size.

Function Keys

Those keys marked F1 to F8, F12, or F15, usually at the top of the keyboard. They are used by software publishers to perform specific functions, which vary with different programs.

Gigabyte

About a billion bytes.

GUI

Pronounced "gooey," this means Graphical User Interface. You do things with little drawings called icons rather than with words. Microsoft Windows and the Macintosh System are both GUIs.

Hard Copy

A printed paper copy.

Hardware

The computer, monitor, keyboard and the other computer devices that you can touch and handle.

HPPCL

Laser printers speak one of two main languages: HPPCL, the Hewlett-Packard Printer Control Language, or PostScript. An HPPCL-speaking printer is fine for most purposes. People who publish a lot of fancy stuff should spring for the extra cost of a PostScript-literate printer. Also at extra cost, many non-PostScript printers can "emulate" (pretend they are) PostScript printers.

Icon

Small pictures which correspond to programs and files and may be used to open those programs.

Interlaced

An interlaced monitor paints only half the screen at a time—every other line—and then it goes back and does the other half. It may flicker, either visibly or subliminally, and the flickering can tire your eyes even if they can't see it. A non-interlaced monitor doesn't paint only half the screen at a time, and consequently doesn't flicker or streak.

IDE

Integrated Drive Electronics. Most PCs have IDE drives, with most of the electronics that run the drive in the actual drive.

Kilobyte

A thousand (actually 1,024) bytes. A double-spaced one-page business letter takes about two kilobytes of memory or storage.

LAN

Local Area Network. Ties nearby computers together to share programs and data.

Laptop

A lightweight, battery-powered computer that unfolds, so that you may work on your lap or carry to a workspace other than your office.

Local Bus

A direct connection between a board and a computer's processor.

Megabyte

A million (actually 1,048,575) bytes. The working memory in your computer takes up four or, better, eight or, better still, sixteen megabytes. The hard disk stores 200 or more megabytes.

Memory-Resident Program

A program that is always available for use at the touch of a key or keys, no matter what other program you are working in.

MIDI

Musical Instrument Digital Interface. With MIDI, you can connect electronic musical instruments to your computer.

Motherboard

The main circuit board inside the box to which everything else is attached.

MPC

Multimedia Personal Computer. Currently MPC2 defines the minimum—and we do mean minimum—standards for a PC to run multimedia.

Multimedia

Computers and programs that can run more than one medium at a time—not just text, but text plus sound, or text plus videos, or text plus sound *and* videos.

Network

Computers connected to share programs and data.

Non-Interlaced

An interlaced monitor paints only half the screen at a time—every other line—and then it goes back and does the other half. It may flicker, either visibly or subliminally, and the flickering can tire your eyes even if they can't see it. A non-interlaced monitor doesn't paint only half the screen at a time, and consequently doesn't flicker or streak.

Numeric Keypad

The separate set of number keys at the far right side of the keyboard. These are especially useful for doing mathematical calculations or working on programs such as spreadsheets.

OCR, or Optical Character Recognition

A scanner-software combination that can transform the graphic image of text into real text, which can be edited with a word processor.

PCMCIA

Personal Computer Memory Card International Association, a group that sets the standards for little PCMCIA cards that are inserted into portable computers (but couldn't think of a catchy name for them).

Paint Program

A graphics program that stores the pieces of a drawing as bits. Also see *bit-mapped fonts*.

Peripheral

Any device, other than keyboard or screen, that you attach to your computer.

Piracy

Stealing software.

Pixel

A picture element—one of the dots that the letters, numbers, squares, and circles on the screen are made of.

Point

The unit of size of a font. A point is about one seventy-second of an inch, so a font an inch tall is seventy-two points.

PostScript

Laser printers speak one of two main languages: HPPCL, the Hewlett-Packard Printer Control Language, or PostScript. An HPPCL-speaking printer is fine for most purposes. People who publish a lot of fancy stuff should spring for the extra cost of a PostScript-literate printer. Also at extra cost, many non-PostScript printers can "emulate"—pretend they are—PostScript printers.

Power Strip

A device with several electrical sockets that allows you to plug many devices into one wall outlet. Be careful not to turn them all on at once.

PPM

Pages per minute. A measure of the speed of a Laser of Inkjet printer. Dot-matrix printers are measured in CPSs.

RAM

Random Access Memory, where programs and information are stored when the power is on. It is random access because the CPU can go directly to where data is stored, as you change directly from channel 2 to channel 7 on a remote control, instead of having to slog through channels 3, 4, 5, and 6, as you do with a rotary dial on a television set.

Relational Database

A database manager that stores its information in several tables. In a client list, the information blanks could be in several different tables. Relational databases are more flexible than flat-file databases, as well as more expensive and often more difficult to use.

ROM

With ROM, Read Only Memory, you can only get information, you can't store new information or change old information. The ROM contains instructions that the computer cannot do without and that must not be changed. ROMs in Macintoshes hold more information than ROMs in PCs.

SCSI

Pronounced *scuzzy*, this means Small Computer System Interface. One of the ways various peripherals, especially hard drives, are attached to computers.

Scalable Fonts

Also called outline fonts, these are characters described by mathematical formulas rather than locked into bit-maps. Their size can be changed on the fly.

Scanner

A peripheral that copies photographs or text onto the computer's disk.

Screen Saver

A program that comes on when your computer has not been used for a specified number of minutes. Screen savers are designed to avoid the remote possibility of burning an unchanged image into the screen. Mostly for fun.

Slots

Spaces inside the main box in which accessory circuit boards are attached to the motherboard.

Software

Computer programs written to perform specified tasks. Software is what makes the hardware function for you.

Spreadsheet

A computer program that automates an accountant's worksheet, automatically changing as new numbers are plugged in.

Surge Suppressor

A device between the wall outlet and computer plug that protects the equipment from damaging electric surges.

SVGA

Super You Know What (VGA), which offers a resolution of 800 by 600 pixels, or 1,024 by 768, or even more. It is crisper than regular VGA, but also slower, unless you have more powerful gear than you need for VGA.

SWM

Single white male.

Trackball

An upside-down mouse.

UPS

Uninterruptable power supply. A device that you plug your hardware into. If your office loses power, the UPS provides at least enough power for you to complete the operation you are working on and close down in a mannerly fashion without losing vital data.

VDT

Video display terminal. Another term for your screen display, or monitor, or CRT.

VGA

Video Graphics Array, a standard in PC monitors and their associated internal computer circuitry that offers a resolution of 640 by 480 pixels. The term is not ordinarily applied to Macintosh monitors, most of which offer at least the same resolution standard, however.

Version Numbers

The first issue of a program is 1.0; the second issue, with a major change, is 2.0. Between 1.0 and 2.0 will be versions with small improvements and small, or not so small, corrections, numbered 1.01 or 1.2 or 1.23. The smart money never buys a version that ends with ".0." The version that ends with ".1" or higher has the worst errors of ".0" fixed. Maybe.

Virus

A software program written with the intention of disrupting your work, damaging files or making your computer like HAL in "2001."

VLF

Very low frequency.

User Groups

Clubs where users of computers and software get together to gossip, exchange information, and bitch.

Windows, windows

Windows with a capital W is short for the program Microsoft Windows. Windows with a small w are framed areas on the computer screen. The Macintosh uses windows but not Windows. Windows uses windows.

Word Processing

It used to be called writing.

INDEX